Active Whole-Class Teaching

Robert Powell

Book Two of the Put Learning First Series

Robert Powell Publications

Published by
Robert Powell Publications
56 Stockton Lane
Stafford. ST17 0JS

First Published 1997
© Robert Powell Publications
ISBN 1 901841 05 7

Acknowledgements
My thanks are due to all the thousands of teachers across the
UK who have inspired me with their stamina, ingenuity and creative thinking.
Particular thanks go to John Murray Publishers, to HMSO and to
Carel Press for permission to reproduce extracts from their publications.

Designed by
Neil Hawkins of Devine Design

Printed in Great Britain by
Redwood Books, Trowbridge, Wiltshire.

For John Ambler

*A valued friend and
an inspiration to us both.*

Contents

Introduction

Every August a bizarre ritual is played out on publication of the examination results. Traditionalists from the *'examinations are easier'* brigade dust off their notes from the previous year and try to find a new way of saying what they have said every year without fail ever since GCSE was introduced. The *'standards are up'* or *'standards are down'* debate misses the point; more students achieving a grade 'A' does not mean the standard for an 'A' has changed, it merely means that more students are achieving the standard. When Roger Bannister became the first person to run a mile in less than four minutes on 6 May 1954, few would have anticipated that the four-minute mile in the 1990s would be quite normal for a high-class club athlete. I am surprised that the traditionalists have not suggested that the track has been made shorter. More students than ever before are setting themselves the target of achieving highly in examinations, and there are no artificial barriers like there were in the days of 'O' Level which used to limit the number of students who could be awarded the top grades.

No, the curriculum offered to students in the UK remains as challenging as ever. Yes there are new courses. In the 1970s Sociology was labelled a *'trendy soft option'*, and now it is the turn of courses like Sports Science whose critics will attack it without even looking at the syllabus. (I'm not a historian but I wonder whether the study of Science was labelled as trendy, progressive nonsense by classicists in the 19th Century.) Sports Science is a rigorous, academic discipline, a course heavy in physiology, theory and conceptual language that is comparable in terms of academic demand with most *'traditional'* courses.

Most courses across the UK will include areas of study that involve complex theory, contain abstract concepts and demand the acquisition of a whole new language (take GNVQ for example!) The curriculum is as demanding as ever and the challenge for the teacher is to find a way to make the courses accessible to students who, even in classes set by ability, will vary in their intellectual and physical skills. Teachers will use a variety of strategies, and one of them will be whole-class teaching, an approach that presents to teachers its own set of challenges.

During the Summer term of 1997, BBC Television screened a feature on security in schools. Towards the end of the programme a police sergeant was filmed talking to a group of six-year-olds about what to do if a stranger approached them.

'I have a question for you,' he said.

Immediately all their hands shot in the air. They didn't yet know what the question was but they all wanted to be first to answer. This phenomenon, which I shall call the *'MeMe'* phase (because children shout out 'me, me') characterises whole-class teaching during the early years of junior school education. This enthusiasm for participation in class teaching does not last. By the age of twelve it has become the *'MeLater'* phase where the brave children are still eager but others wait to be asked.

By the age of fourteen it is replaced with the *'NotMe'* phase which will be familiar to most teachers. During this phase whenever a question is asked a small number of students (always the same ones) put their hands in the air (I call these the *'volunteers'*). The teacher gratefully takes their responses, thanks them and then picks on three or four more (the *'conscripts'*). The teacher will usually select different conscripts each lesson and such students breathe a sigh of relief when they have been chosen because they know that their contribution for the month is over.

By the age of seventeen a new phenomenon has emerged; it is the *'DoItForMe'* phase where students, particularly those on A Level and Highers courses, find participation in class teaching a real ordeal, where the *'any questions'* request is met with blank stares and where everything the teacher says is written down. Most teachers of this age group will have met the student who sees participation as unnecessary because the teacher will *'do it for me'*. Such passivity is not so common in classes studying GNVQ or vocational courses but even here participation in whole-class teaching is not universal.

Strangely, the *'MeMe'* phase returns in Adult Education where the more mature student, after an initial nervousness, is often eager to participate. During the 1970s I taught O level Sociology to a group of thirty adults, mostly women. For one session with this group I invited a friend of mine, a woman with radical feminist views, to do a presentation on Women's Rights. At one point in her talk she put forward the view that all children ought to be brought up by professional nannies organised and funded by state bureaucracy, freeing women to have the same access to a career structure as men. She pointed out to the group that such an experiment had taken place in Russia just after the First World War. She got no further. At this point one of the women in the class shot to her feet and shouted:

'And it didn't bloody well work, did it?'

The floodgates opened and the presenter was submerged in a torrent of argument and debate where everyone wanted to participate. The two-hour session passed very quickly and in the pub later one of the group said to me *'That's why I go to evening classes'*. I decided to offer the same experience to my Sixth Form A Level group and looked forward eagerly to the lesson. When the speaker reached the point in the talk which had led to the outburst in the evening class she was also interrupted:

'Excuse me, how do you spell 'bureaucracy'?'

The differing responses of the seventeen-year-old and the adult has even led to some FE colleges teaching adults and teenagers on the same courses in different classes.

I have worked with teachers from all sectors of education and they recognise the various phases that I have outlined. There are, of course, teachers who are able to encourage and sustain participation, whatever the age group of the students, and colleagues will often say to such people

'How do you get them to talk like that? They are so dead in my lessons.'

That is why I think a book like this is needed. Teachers from all phases of education ask for guidance on these issues. How do you encourage students to ask questions? How do you persuade them to share their ideas publicly in a whole-class situation? How do you involve everybody in a question/answer session? How do you build the confidence of the shy or control the enthusiasm of the dominant personalities? Good whole-class teachers will do all of these things yet it is remarkable how many experienced teachers find this the most challenging aspect of their job. Of equal concern is the number of student teachers who come into the profession without a working knowledge of the techniques that are required for effective whole-class teaching. I have worked with hundreds of schools on in-sevice days where ideas on such techniques are shared, and in all of these schools Newly Qualified or Associate Teachers approach me and ask why such ideas are not taught in their teacher training courses.   I am not one to damn teacher training on such flimsy evidence, but my hunch is that such techniques are being taught in only the best colleges or university courses, not all, and the reason is that too few teacher trainers themselves have a command of the techniques of whole-class teaching. I believe that teacher training courses need to place a greater emphasis on such techniques, and if, as I argued in Book One, in-service training is improved, effective whole-class teaching will become part of the repertoire of *all* teachers.

In saying this I do not share the views of those who argue that whole-class teaching should be the dominant strategy used by teachers. Good teachers will use a wide variety of strategies at different times to suit different purposes. Whole-class teaching will be used frequently, but as I argued in Book One, its use will vary from short bursts of five minutes at various intervals during one lesson to a whole hour of exposition. The important point is that effective whole-class teaching involves a range of different skills and techniques. It is often characterised as a simple matter of standing in front of a willing class and instructing the students in the finer points of the subject in hand. This type of whole-class teaching is quite common - I know this because I have read many inspection reports for secondary schools which include comments such as:

- *The teaching strategies adopted offered few opportunities for developing independent skills*

- *There was a lack of differentiation in the pace and style of delivery*

- *The teaching failed to challenge the more able students*

- *There was an over-reliance on teacher exposition*

- *The teacher's dominance gave little oppportunity for class or small group discussion*

- *The class teaching relied too heavily on dictation and copying from the blackboard.*

The call from various groups for more whole-class teaching is totally inappropriate for many secondary schools; they do not need *more* whole-class teaching but *better* and more effective whole-class teaching. In the primary school sector there may be a case for more whole-class teaching but if teachers from this phase simply adopt the poor practice that is found in some secondary classrooms, then all that will be achieved will be to replace one form of poor teaching with another.   That type of error has happened before in British Education. I remember in the late 1970s and early 1980s the call for more resource-based learning where information that would have been presented orally by the teacher was produced in booklets written by staff in countless curriculum development centres. This revolution changed the face of many classrooms; instead of being bored to death by *teacher talk* students were bored to death by *worksheets*. This type of mistake should not be allowed to happen again. The perceived failures of whole-class teaching in the 1970s led to that revolution, and School Inspectors all over the UK have, for more than twenty-five years, warned of the dangers of an over-reliance on didactic methods.   But in some schools this advice led to the abandonment of whole-class teaching with the resulting '*death by worksheet'* syndrome. If there is a feeling that the pendulum swung too far then headteachers, governors, advisers, inspectors, task-force groups and Secretaries of State for Education must ensure that the current call for more whole-class teaching is tempered with the acceptance that other teaching and learning strategies must still be used. Good teachers will adopt whole-class teaching at appropriate moments and on other occasions will choose well-organised group work, independent learning, practical activity or problem-solving. This book is designed to help teachers make their whole-class teaching more effective and more exciting, not to promote this as being the only worthwhile approach. The book is not a step-by-step recipe which all teachers should follow blindly, but more of a *menu* of ideas, which like all menus, teachers will select from to suit the mood or occasion. I expect teachers to regard some of the ideas as *'old hat'*, some as interesting, some exciting and some *'off the wall'* (or for some, *'off the planet'*). Some teachers will use the ideas as described, some will use bits of them, some will adapt them, some will be stimulated to produce their own ideas. Whole-class teaching can be an exciting, stimulating and effective experience where students not only learn a great deal but are left wanting to know or do more. Achieving this with large classes, inadequate resources and little time for planning is not easy; it requires energy, confidence and a great deal of skill. This book is a genuine attempt to support teachers in the development of such confidence and such skills. As for the *energy*, readers will have to look back to Chapters Six and Seven of Book One if that is their key concern!

The book has a simple structure:

Chapter One sets out some of the preparation work that teachers are advised to consider if they want their whole-class teaching to run smoothly and successfully.

Chapter Two examines some of the techniques that teachers can use when whole-class teaching is being used for the instruction of new knowledge, concepts or skills.

Chapter Three focusses on those occasions when teachers are trying to develop thinking skills or to consolidate understanding through whole-class question/answer sessions.

Chapter Four suggests techniques that can be used when teachers are using whole-class teaching at the end of a topic where assessing, reviewing or revising is the main agenda.

Chapter Five looks at the classroom itself and how the layout can be adapted to suit a variety of teaching and learning strategies.

Unlike Book One, it is not designed to be read from cover to cover. Chapter One will be important to the inexperienced teacher because it introduces some important principles which many more-experienced colleagues will see as normal good practice, but other chapters can be dipped into at random.

Finally, please remember that a good idea can often be adapted to fit any situation, any age group and any subject. Techniques set out in Chapter Two on instruction might well work brilliantly in a whole-class revision lesson; a strategy that is described in Chapter Three on questioning might be adapted successfully by a teacher for use in an introduction to a new topic; a game that is being used by a teacher to encourage questioning with a group of adults on a vocational course might work perfectly well with a group of five-year-olds. Most of the ideas are transferable between Primary, Secondary, Sixth Form and Further or Higher Education. (I hope lecturers will forgive the generic use of the word *teacher*. I felt it would be clumsy constantly to write teacher/lecturer.) The simple message is: look at each idea, ask yourself if it can be adapted, think freely, think widely, be brave and share your experiences with others.

Chapter One   1

Preparing the Ground

This chapter will examine:

- Preparation

- Ground Rules

- Classroom Organisation

Preparing the Ground

We have all met teachers who have that ability to make whole-class teaching seem easy. They walk into the room and instantly command the attention of all the students. Every word they utter is listened to with rapt attention, and questioning of the class leads to a forest of hands in the air, vying for the attention of the teacher. The qualities that make such teachers so successful vary; they may be humorous, sympathetic, dramatic or eccentric, but their skills will be difficult to define and impossible to categorise because others who are strict or humorous fail to achieve the same level of response from students. This leads some to suggest that good teachers are born not made, that the skill of class teaching cannot be taught. I do not subscribe to that. Of course you cannot give teachers charisma that they are not born with, but there are tricks of the trade that can be learned, techniques that can be practised and organisational skills that can be acquired. This chapter looks at the issue of organisation and preparation because if you observe skilled class teachers at work you marvel at how organised they are, how the students seem to know what to do, how unwritten rules seem to operate as if by magic; the lesson seems to run by clockwork. It is not magic or clockwork but careful planning, summarised with three key headings:

- Preparation

- Ground rules

- Classroom organisation.

Preparation

Good whole-class teaching is rarely just teacher talk. Most successful lessons will involve a good deal of thought and prior planning. The following checklist highlights some of the important preparation that precedes and underpins the effective whole-class lesson.

1. If the class is a new one, the teacher has prepared a seating plan listing the names of students and placed it so that she can refer to it when necessary.

2. The teacher is clear about the learning objectives for the lesson and will have a clear picture of the knowledge, understanding or skills that the students will have acquired by the end.

3. The teacher has prepared an outline of the various phases of the lesson and of the strategies that he will empty at each stage.

4. Where appropriate the teacher has thought about and prepared concrete examples that might be used to illustrate key concepts or skills that will be introduced during the lesson.

5. The resources that will be needed have been identified, collected, labelled and made easily accessible.

6. Audio-visual resources (eg OHTs) have been prepared or collected.

7. Handouts, if needed, have been prepared in sufficient quantities, and if there are more than one they are clearly labelled or colour-coded.

8. Equipment that will be needed has been collected and checked (eg focus for OHP).

9. A summary of the oral instructions that will be given during the lesson are displayed in the classroom.

10. The follow-up tasks or homework are prepared and ready to display or distribute.

Ground Rules

One of the reasons that some lessons seem to run by clockwork is that the teacher has established and shared with the students a clear set of expectations, rules and procedures; I shall refer to these as *ground rules*. Some should be whole-school (where this is the case it is indicated in brackets) and such ground rules will be more effective if they have been discussed and agreed by all staff, students, parents and governors. Others, such as those that relate to safety, in subjects such as Physical Education, Technology and Science, will be departmental, and others will be the personal preferences of individual teachers. In all cases the purpose for the ground rules should be explained to all students, and if possible, agreed by them. The ground rules that follow relate entirely to those that can be used to support effective whole-class teaching and concentrate on two broad areas:

(a) Ground rules that encourage participation

(b) Ground rules for the use of groups in whole-class teaching.

Many of them have been used by generations of teachers, indeed some are based on ideas in published texts - two of the best being Michael Marland's classic, *The Craft of the Classroom*, and Philip Waterhouse's ageless handbook, *Classroom Management*. Other ideas have come from colleagues that I have met or worked with over the years who have that knack of coming up with ideas that make you think *'That's so simple. Why didn't I think of that before?'*

The selection of ground rules included in this chapter are designed to be used selectively by teachers but they might form the basis of team or departmental discussion and might be used in the formulation of policies. Almost certainly, they will be used to generate other ideas.

Many teachers who have talked with me over the years on the challenges of whole-class teaching have begun the conversation with *'How do you overcome the problem of...?'* This will be the starting point for this section: common problems faced by teachers of all phases. Each set of problems will be followed by a range of ground rules adopted by teachers in an attempt to overcome the difficulties they are facing. It is worth emphasising here, however, that ground rules that are simply written policies, filed away and ignored, will quickly become worthless. Say what you mean and mean what you say!

Ground Rules that Encourage Participation

Common Problems

- Some students are reluctant to participate in case their responses are ridiculed by the teacher or, more likely, other students.
- Some students feel threatened in the free-for-all oral lesson by those who are assertive, confident, aggressive or simply loud.
- Some students hold back because they are likely to be called names if they participate willingly - *'square'*, *'boffin'*, *'egg-head'* spring to mind, but conventions and terms of abuse change over time.
- Some girls are reluctant to speak in classes where boys dominate class discussion and question/answer sessions. Occasionally, these gender roles are reversed.
- Some classes are dominated by a small group of students who can be relied on to participate; both teachers and other students are happy for this to continue.

Ground Rules on Participation

Ground Rule 1 It is agreed that all contributions will be valued and celebrated; no put-downs will be allowed from the teacher or other students. (Whole-School/College ground rule)

Ground Rule 2 The teacher acts as a chairperson and all contributions must go through the chair. No shouting out is allowed and the chair will invite contributions at her discretion.

Ground Rule 3 The same as Ground Rule 2 above only students are asked to perform the role of chairperson on a rota basis, and while the teacher might generate the question or issue the chair decides who will be invited to respond. Some teachers who have used this approach have two students controlling the lesson; the chairperson and a secretary who makes a note of whose turn it is to speak next.

Ground Rule 4 Each student is allocated a number (eg 1-30) and in lessons when many students want to contribute the chairperson allocates numbers and allows students to speak when their numbers are called.

Ground Rule 5 All students are each allocated a number by the teacher which they keep as their reference for the duration of their time with that teacher. The teacher has a pack of cards with numbers on, the cards are shuffled and each person contributes when their number appears at the top of the pack.

Ground Rule 6 Each student who responds to a question nominates the next student to speak. (See also the game *Nomination* on page 62)

Ground Rule 7 The teacher uses the Snowball Technique to ensure that all students participate. (See page 55 for an explanation of this technique.)

Using groups within whole-class teaching

One of the best ways to ensure participation within whole-class teaching is to divide the class into a number of small groups (see the description of support groups, ground rule 8 below, and the Snowball Technique on page 55). The use of small groups in this way has a number of benefits but brings with it a number of potential problems. Ground rules for the use of small groups in whole-class teaching are therefore very important.

Common Problems When Using Groups

- The group is often dominated by one or two students with the others doing very little. The teacher can never be sure of who has contributed.
- Some groups talk about everything but the task in hand.
- Some students in groups spend their time winding each other up, arguing or irritating each other and the teacher is diverted into dealing with behaviour.
- Some groups finish more quickly than others and then get restless when they have to wait.
- Some groups spend too long sorting out what has to be done and waste time debating who is to do what.
- Some classrooms have large, inflexible furniture (eg some science laboratories or technology classrooms), and students are forced to sit around tables in groups for all activities. When

whole-class teaching takes place half the students have their backs to the teacher and this can lead to lack of concentration or unacceptable behaviour.

Ground Rules for Working With Groups

Ground Rule 8 Teachers organise their classes into small *support groups.* Support groups are groups within a class, four perhaps, whose task is to provide support for individual members. The make-up of the group will be decided by the teacher, not by the students, and the group will be chosen on simple criteria: *will members of this group be able to provide support to each other when they are required to do so?* A support group of seven-year-olds, therefore, might consist of two good readers and two who find reading difficult (pairs of friends are often a good starting point for forming a support group). At A Level or Highers, for example, the support group might be formed on the basis of skill or confidence levels. Friendship groups might work for some students but will be a disaster for others, and so teachers must use a large dose of common sense and sensitivity in choosing groups. Teachers must also accept that with some classes they will be changed regularly to reflect the fluctuating relationships that characterise adolescence.

Ground Rule 9 Support groups, other groups and seating arrangements are chosen by the teacher not by the students.

(Whole-school ground rule. Teachers of adults in Further or Higher Education will have to use their discretion with this ground rule.)

Ground Rule 10 It is made clear from the beginning that in any group work each person must fulfil a role, eg chairperson, scribe, spokesperson. Roles must be rotated.

Ground Rule 11 In short periods of small group discussion the role of the scribe is to record ideas or responses from individual members of the group. The initials of the person whose idea it was are placed alongside each idea so that the teacher can check on the level of participation.

Ground Rule 12 A very strict time limit is placed on each small group activity including, for example, 30 seconds to sort out who is doing what within the group. One role of the chairperson is to ensure that the deadlines are met. Some teachers have a system for limiting the time given and although the ideas are diverse all seem to have the effect of helping students to stay on the task.

- One teacher in Scotland plays a recording of *Mission Impossible* - when the music finishes the time is up. (See also the Chapter 4, Example No 32)
- Another teacher uses an egg timer.
- One uses a kitchen timer.
- Several teachers have decided to use gongs.
- One music teacher plays a short tune on the piano reminiscent of the music which used to accompany the action episodes in the 1920s silent films.

Ground Rule 13 In any classroom where students are seated around tables in groups everyone must turn around and face the teacher when whole-class instruction or discussion is taking place. (Whole-School/College)

The classroom layout itself is an important factor in effective whole-class teaching and can have a major influence on the teacher's ability to switch easily and without disruption from one activity to another. Logically, therefore, an analysis of classroom layout should appear in this chapter on setting the scene. I have decided, however, to look at the classroom at the end of the book because the chapters that follow examine a wide range of possible active class teaching techniques. When colleagues have read these they will be in a better position to evaluate the importance of classroom layout.

Chapter Two

Whole-Class Teaching
for Instruction

This chapter will examine:

- Clear Purpose

- Start from the Familiar

- Visual Aids

- Note-Giving

- Handouts

- Clarity and Understanding

Whole-Class Teaching Used for Instruction

Traditionalists who have been calling for a return to that golden age when students sat in rows and listened to teachers instructing them need not have worried. In secondary schools in particular such approaches have never gone away. I remember fondly a colleague of mine during the so-called progressive 70s telling me he used *'discovery learning'*;

'If the students talk while I am teaching they discover that they get belted.'

Many teachers, as any headteacher will tell you, have worked professionally throughout the 70s, 80s and 90s politely ignoring the latest innovation being thrust at them. Indeed, a colleague of mine running an in-service day for a school was criticised by a self-professed cynic who claimed to have '25 years of experience'. His headteacher put it differently:

'He's had one year's experience repeated 25 times!'

No, whole-class teaching is alive and well. One of the most common uses of whole-class teaching is in instruction where the teacher either through talk, note-giving or handouts, and often a combination of all three, introduces to the class new knowledge, concepts, skills or processes.

For many teachers the process of whole-class instruction is simple: they stand or sit in front of the class, occasionally patrolling the classroom, and talk. Periodically they will say *'Is everyone clear about that?'* All the students nod. What the teacher fails to realise is that the class contains *three* separate groups of students nodding for different reasons. The students in the first group are nodding because they understand. The students in the second group are nodding because they genuinely *think* they understand. As an example of this I recall the story of the farmer from the United States who visited the UK for a farming conference. In the bar in the evening he struck up a conversation with a farmer from the UK:

'Back in the States', he boasted, *'if I want to inspect my land I get in my Jeep on Monday morning and don't get back until the following Friday.'*

'I know how you feel,' said the farmer from the UK, *'I once had a Land Rover like that.'*

The students in the third group are nodding because they *don't* understand; in fact, they are utterly confused. But they know that if they own up to this fact some teachers will shout at them for not listening, and in other classrooms the more sympathetic teacher will be happy to help them but it will be other students who will shout abuse. This *'nodding'* ritual and the close relation the *'shaking of heads'* ritual that follows the 'any questions' request from the teacher, are played to identical rules in countless classrooms around the UK and probably worldwide. This phenomenon is not confined to younger students, students with learning difficulties or students with low motivation. It will be true of A Level or Highers classes, of the top set in a setted situation and even of teachers themselves faced with the same questions from a trainer on an in-service course. The topic, in the mind of the teacher, has been *'covered'* but in many instances the learning will be superficial and the deeper understanding that is required for longer-term achievement is missing.

The first task for teachers keen to improve the effectiveness of their whole-class instruction, therefore, is to recognise the realities of such situations; there will always be students who for one reason or another fail to stay with teachers as they progress through the phase of the planned instruction. It might be a problem of language, poor concentration, lack of motivation or basic gaps in understanding; in dictation it might simply be that some students write more slowly than others. Even well-motivated and confident students will only be able to concentrate on what the teacher is saying for so long. Once teachers accept that this is the reality then strategies can be adopted which help students to understand what is going on, to concentrate on what the teacher is saying, to enjoy the experience and ultimately to learn as much as possible from the lesson.

The section that follows sets out a number of strategies that will support teachers in whole-class instruction. Many teachers will find that much of what follows is no more than their own good practice, but some of the ideas may enhance the work of even highly successful whole-class teachers and they will certainly provide support to those who are new to the profession or to those who find this aspect of their work a challenge. The strategies are based on six basic principles of whole-class instruction:

1 Clear purpose: that all students share with the teacher a clear understanding of the purpose and scope of the lesson.

2 Start from the familiar: that difficult theory and challenging concepts can sometimes be explained by starting from the concrete experiences of students.

3 Visual aids: that teacher talk is supported by the use of visual aids.

4 Note-giving: that note-giving is interactive and requires students to make sense of the information.

5 Handouts: that handouts are used to reduce the time spent on dictation but care is taken to ensure that they are not simply filed 'for later'.

6 Clarity and understanding: that clarity and understanding are ensured in a non-threatening and participative manner.

1 Clear Purpose

One of the first principles in effective whole-class teaching is that the teacher has a clear purpose which is shared with the students. This principle is not new and is probably one of the criteria school inspectors look for in any inspection system anywhere in the world. The problem is that the principle is easier than the practice. The example below illustrates the point:

An inspector for Modern Languages sat at the back of the room in a class of bottom set fourteen-year-olds. Two minutes into the lesson one of the back row students turned to the inspector and the following conversation took place:

    Student: *'Do you speak French?'*
    Inspector: *'Oui.'*
    Student: *'Do you speak German?'*
    Inspector: *'Ja.'*
    Student: *'Which one's this, then?'*

Not all students will be as confused as this one but it is remarkably difficult sometimes to explain the purpose of a lesson in a way that students understand.   Yet it must be done, particularly if the teacher wants to encourage student participation. Students who are confident and whose self-esteem is intact are more likely to participate, and this confidence starts with being clear about the purpose of the lesson. Both Michael Marland and Philip Waterhouse in their respective books advise teachers to *'tell them what you are going to say, say it and then tell them what you have said'*.

I believe that teachers may need to go further than that. Those of us who have tried to put together a self-assembly MFI wardrobe will know that a crucial resource is the exploded diagram that is somewhere in the box containing the furniture. This tells us whether it is tall and thin or long and flat, and without it the bits would seem like a jigsaw for members of Mensa - the one with no picture on the lid. Teachers must, therefore, give students the big picture from the start, or what Ausubal called an *'advance organiser'*. The examples that follow will illustrate what I mean.

The Advance Organiser   Example 1

I once observed Philip Waterhouse, the author of *Classroom Management*, teaching a class of eleven-year-olds during the period when he was Director of the Avon Resources For Learning Project. It was a Humanities lesson and the topic was *The Port of Bristol*. The topic was due to last some four weeks or more, and, as an evaluator of the Project, I was due to observe and evaluate the way Philip integrated whole-class teaching with resource-based learning approaches. I was present for the introductory lesson when Philip presented to the class his *'advance organiser'* - a summary in advance of what the class would learn about in the new topic. He took the class through the history of Bristol and its port using a series of overheads designed to give an outline snapshot of the city at various periods in its history. With the help of the class he related the changes that the city went through, adding words and illustrations to the overheads as the story unfolded. Key words like *'settlement'* were explained and then displayed on cards on the classroom wall.

Towards the end of the double lesson the students were asked to draw in their exercise books a time line or flow chart based on what they had learned so far, the task to be completed for homework. This, Philip explained to them, would act as an advance organiser for the lessons that were to follow when they would be looking at each historical phase in more depth. The students in the class were spellbound (and so was I). It was one of the finest examples of whole-class teaching that I have ever been privileged to observe. The lessons that followed, which included some very high quality work in small groups, owed much to the enthusiasm and understanding that were generated in that first whole-class lesson.

This example illustrates a number of important issues:
- ➡ By the end of the introduction students had a clear overview of the topic that they were to study for several weeks.
- ➡ The involvement of students in building the *'big picture'* of what the topic entailed secured their interest and attention.
- ➡ The timeline/flow chart activity at the end had three benefits: (1) it helped to reinforced the key messages of the class teaching; (2) it allowed students to start lesson two with a worthwhile product from lesson one; (3) it aided longer-term memory by providing a visual summary of the key points of the lesson. (See section that follows on the use of visual aids.)
- ➡ The display of key words was part of an on-going process of building language.

• • • • •

2 Start from the Familiar

One of the best ways to help students cope with abstract ideas, challenging concepts or difficult theory is to start with their own experience and not with the theory. A skilled teacher can use concrete experiences or prior knowledge as a vehicle for moving into the abstract, for defining concepts and for formulating rules or theory. As a young teacher I faced the challenges of ROSLA (the Raising of the School Leaving Age in 1973). Many of my ROSLA students claimed they were 'no good' at Mathematics, but were extremely good at mental arithmetic when they were playing darts, and they knew exactly what their winnings would be (less 25% tax) when the 50p they had placed on the 3.30 at Ascot came in at 13/8 on!

Using Prior Knowledge   Example 2

I worked with the Special Needs team in a Further Education College in Surrey who were working with a group of students on a basic life skills course. All the students had severe learning difficulties and although behaviour was not a problem, motivation and self-esteem were both low. One of the topics in the course was the use of money and the ability to give and receive change in a shopping situation. The teachers knew that any mention of mathematics would result in groans from the students so they introduced the topic by telling the class that as part of this topic they would have to set up and run their own shop in the class, selling fruit, crisps, biscuits and sweets. In order for this to be possible they would have to learn first how to count and multiply in the units of money - 2s, 5s, 10s, 20s, 50s and 100s.

Before any direct teaching on this, however, the teachers asked the students which of these counting skills they could already do, and then told them to pair up so that those, for example, who could already count in 5s were able to coach those who could not. A short period of intense activity followed and then the teacher brought the whole class together for some formal instruction on the necessary skills, and then set a series of text book exercises to reinforce the learning. The motivation for this phase of the lesson was good and as a result participation in the class teaching was high.

This example highlights other aspects of good practice:
- ➡ The activity that would be the climax of a series of lessons on mathematical skills was introduced at the start, giving a purpose to the teaching that followed.
- ➡ The paired activity enabled the students to show what they already knew and an opportunity to help others provided a welcome boost to their self-esteem and confidence.
- ➡ Using students' prior learning as a starting point meant that in the formal teaching that followed confidence was high and participation was ensured.
- ➡ The conceptual link between counting in 5s and giving change was established.

• • • • •

For many students making the jump from concrete operations to abstract thought can be too daunting. The journey from handling objects to visualising them, to recognising and interpreting them and linear representations can be hazardous.

Introducing map contours in Geography is such a journey. It is not just a case of students with special needs having difficulties - many students find it hard to make sense of winding, numbered lines on a Two-dimensional O S Map.

Often the pace of a lesson can be too fast with not enough time for students to assimilate information and knowledge, practise a new skill and build their self-confidence.

Imagine receiving holiday picture-postcards where the mountains, canyons and lakes had been replaced by narrow bands of numbered lines. It might take a while to work out what your friends had seen. But here is one possible route to teaching, learning and understanding map contours.

| Example 3 | From the Concrete to the Abstract (Contours) |

Stage 1
A roller coaster travels up and down like a journey across high and lowland. The views we see from high land are different from the views we see on lowland. From high land we can look down and see a plan view.

Stage

A face on its side has high and low parts. Some parts are flat, some parts are steep. If the face on its side is a geographical face - like an island - we call the view we can see a cross-section.

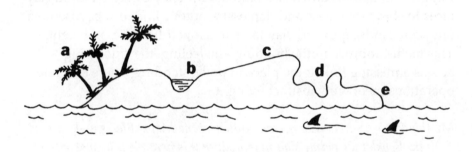

The eye of the face becomes a lake, the nose an escarpment, the mouth a canyon, the chin a cliff and the hair a forest. When we look at an Ordnance Survey map we are always looking down and seeing a plan view. On these maps the ups and downs are shown by lines. These lines are called contour lines. Contour lines join places of the same height and can show us which parts of a map are flat and which parts are steep. We can show the ups and downs of a face in the same way by drawing the face as a plan view and by adding contour lines.

Stage 3

Contour lines drawn close together show parts of the face which are steep. Lines wide apart show parts which are flat.

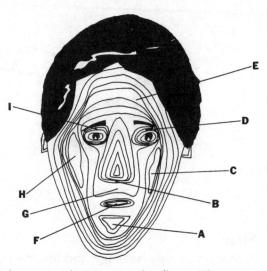

When students use an O S map they are able to run their fingers along the lines and trace the ups and downs to places where the lines run close together (in bands) - the steeps - and to places where the lines are drawn wide apart - the flats. Then, using modelling clay, students can mould pieces of landscape in 3D form to run up and down and flatten out. They can also mould clay faces to show steepness and flatness. Contour lines can be inscribed onto clay landscapes and clay faces to show differences in height. This tactile approach - the building, the feeling, the smoothing - acts as a missing link at the place in understanding where concrete operations meet with abstract thought.

My thanks to Andrew McPherson, author of the Maps, Places and Faces Activity Booklet for permission to reproduce this here. It is available from Cutting Edge Publications on 01208 872337 along with a host of other teacher-friendly resources for English, Humanities and Special Needs.

● ● ● ● ●

3 Visual Aids

The research on how people learn and on how the brain works suggests that humans have multiple intelligences. Howard Gardner, Professor of Education at Harvard University, argues that there are seven groupings of ability or skills which form human intelligences. These are: Linguistic, Mathematical, Visual and Spatial, Musical, Interpersonal, Intrapersonal and Kinesthetic. (Readers who would like to know a little more about each of these should refer to a book called 'Accelerated Learning in the Classroom' by Alistair Smith.)

Some students (and indeed some teachers) will have preferences in the ways in which they learn. Those who need to see ideas, who tend to think in pictures, will suffer if all knowledge, concepts or skills are introduced only in oral or written form. Such students will benefit if they can not only hear the technical language spoken by the teacher but see it on the wall as a word or an illustration. They will benefit also if the structure of the lesson is not only explained but displayed, if the conceptual links between different characters, chemicals, products or events are not only discussed but are the subject of a visual mapping exercise.

Visual representation of Understanding   Example 4

In this example students have to study the information in the text book to decide why the Tsarist Regime collapsed in 1917. They have to show their understanding by drawing connect lines between the different causes (e.g. line A in top picture) and recording them on the notebook (bottom picture).

This example is a useful illustration of a number of key principles:

➡ The teacher uses the illustration to give students a 'big picture' of the topic.

➡ The pictorial representation of the learning will enable some to visualise the themes, concepts, examples and vocabulary that have been explored.

➡ The need to participate in identifying the key links and evidence and then in adding lines to the diagram helps to maintain the motivation and concentration of the students.

This example is from Ben Walsh's Modern World History Teacher's Resource Book. The activities in this book are the best that I have seen in any published text book and are transferable to any subject and any age group. My thanks to John Murray, the publishers, for permission to reproduce it here.

• • • • •

4 Giving Notes

During the 1980s in England, Wales and Northern Ireland successive reports from HMI were critical of teaching in sixth forms, and colleagues from Scotland assure me that similar concerns have been expressed there with regard to Highers.

> *' ...in more than half the lessons seen in sixth forms students spent a considerable proportion of their time as passive recipients of information: little opportunity was provided for discussion or the interchange of ideas and they undertook little independent reading and lacked appropriate study strategies. On many occasions the style of teaching - lecture presentations, the dictation of copious notes and the practice of examination answers - left little scope for students to participate.'*

> *(Secondary Schools. An Appraisal by HMI. HMSO 1988)*

In the mid 1990s successive annual reports from Ofsted have generally been very complimentary about teaching in sixth forms and I find this intriguing; has the practice changed or the criteria for inspection? To use a phrase from the magazine Private Eye, *'I think we should be told'*.

Whatever the answer to this conundrum, the fact remains that note-giving and dictation are still widely used as a form of whole-class instruction, particularly in secondary schools and frequently with students in the post-16 age group.   Dictation, to me, is one of the most wasteful uses of professional expertise that I can think of, second only to spending hours during the Summer Term invigilating examinations. In the worst cases dictation consists merely of moving information from one place (the teacher's notes) to another place (the students' folders). Neither party has to think, and in many cases students are more concerned with recording accurately what is said than understanding the meaning or significance of the words; real understanding and application are postponed until later. Many teachers have confessed to me during my in-service work with schools that they agree with my sentiments but continue to give notes in that way. They cite a number of reasons:

- There is so much content to cover and note-giving is the most effective way to ensure that students have the key information in their folders.

- The students demand it. Many of us will have experienced that marvellous debate within a sixth form lesson only to be asked at the end: *'Are we going to do some work next lesson? We didn't get any notes today!'*

- There are not enough books for all students to be able to make their own notes from the sources used by the teacher.

- The cost of photocopying the notes for distribution as handouts is prohibitive.

- The Catch 22 where teachers spoon-feed the students 'to make sure that the notes are done' and students fail to improve their note-making skills because the teachers 'do it for you'.

For the majority of teachers such concerns are real and not an excuse used to justify poor teaching. Many post-16 students left to their own devices will not make good notes; the squeeze on funding does make teachers cautious in the purchase of books or in the photocopying of handouts; content in courses is daunting. But the most important resource available to both teachers and students is time. Time spent by a highly trained professional reading out notes is an inefficient use of time. Students in sixth forms are renowned for the poor use of private study (or as they call it *'free periods'*).

In Chapter Two of Book One I argued strongly for greater structure in the planning of tasks and assignments, including those for private study. If teachers prepared study guides for independent study they could transform the use of private study and use valuable time efficiently. Such guides would identify the purpose of the activity, highlight appropriate resources and references, provide prompts to key issues, demand a product of some kind, and would lead to an audience when the class reconvened. Students who study A Level, for example, are timetabled typically for between four and five hours per week. Structured private study in the way that I have outlined would enable students to be timetabled for eight hours per week, five of which were with a teacher and three as structured private study. Some of the pressure on teachers would be relieved and they would be able to make better use of their professional skills in dialogue with students - supporting, challenging, cajoling, clarifying, problem-solving; dictating notes comes a pretty poor second to that list! In Further and Higher Education where students traditionally have more private study or flexible learning, it is absolutely essential that students develop the skills of using time profitably.

I make no apologies for this pretty direct attack on the style of note-giving that I have so far portrayed in this chapter. Note-giving, however, is not like that in some classrooms: students are *not* passive, teachers *do* make use of their intellectual skills, learning is *not* postponed until later and time *is* used efficiently.

Example 5	Using a Shorthand Approach

Some teachers encourage their students to develop a type of shorthand where they use abbreviations, symbols and simple illustrations rather than the longhand copying of everything the teacher says. This means that students listen, make sense of the words, and then record the meaning using a personal code. Private study can then be used to add to the shorthand in a way that will be useful in the preparation of assignments. When examinations loom, the reverse process happens; students turn their long notes into a set of key ideas, words or symbols which can be more easily recalled in the pressure of the examination hall.

11 Abbreviations

Clear and accurate abbreviations are used widely to save time and space when writing notes. In some books and articles the words or phrases which are used frequently are written out at the beginning of the article and then abbreviated afterwards.

Some students write notes with connecting words missing:

Save time + space, be careful when reading notes, interpret accurately.

Another method of abbreviating notes is to leave out the vowels:

y cn stll rd ths bt y may nd sm vwls

Match the abbreviations in the boxes below with their corresponding words in the list.

∴	%	pp	NB	cf	op cit
ibid	et al	@	∵	ie	♀
min	h	c1475	C19	♂	"

m	kg	s	V	°C	Cal	°F
l	Ar	Mr	ρ	log	≥	
>	ln	<	λ	J		

This example is taken from Strategies for Studying, by Mike Cotes and Chas White. It is a superb book on study skills for post-16 students. My thanks to Carel Press for permission to reproduce this here.

Using a Template for Notes   Example 6

Another successful approach is to use a template for the notes that are to be recorded like the one below. It might be in the form of a handout or on an OHP. The template also acts as an advance organiser. The teacher explains that each of the sections on the template will be examined in turn and that there will be three stages to each section:

Stage 1 The teacher talks about each one, outlining the issues and evidence while the students make sketch notes, possibly using a shorthand style as described in Example 5.

Stage 2 Small groups or pairs try to agree the key points of that section.

Stage 3 The teacher negotiates with the groups an agreed set of key points which are recorded using the headings on the template. The decision to use a template such as the one illustrated here has a number of advantages:

Planning

Before you write your answer look through the text and sources on pages 17–21. Then use the table below to make brief notes about the points in your report, including in each case the sources, sections or page numbers where you found relevant information. This will help you to organise your writing and ensure that you don't simply copy the text.

	Note down the points you want to make and the source, section or page number where you found relevant information for this			
The successes and failures of the various plans				
The important battles which have taken place				
The new lessons being learnt about warfare				
The casualties				
The morale of the troops				

Now you can prepare your report for the general public. Use the completed table to lightly cross out the items you will not be telling the public.

© JOHN MURRAY   *GCSE Modern World History*

1 The template provides students with the 'big picture'.

2 The note-giving has been interactive, not just dictation.

3 The students go through phases where they are required to listen, to reflect, to discuss and to draw conclusions. This process is likely to aid interpretation, understanding and recall.

4 The negotiation between pairs or small groups facilitates peer tutoring - often the best person to help is a fellow student because teachers sometimes find the topic so easy that they make unwarranted assumptions or fail to recognise an ambiguity.

From Modern World History by Ben Walsh. My thanks to John Murray for permission to reproduce this here. (See also Example 4.)

• • • • •

The Visual mapping of Notes   Example 7

In this example the student has presented the notes visually, drawing connections and highlighting key ideas with a series of illustrations and words.

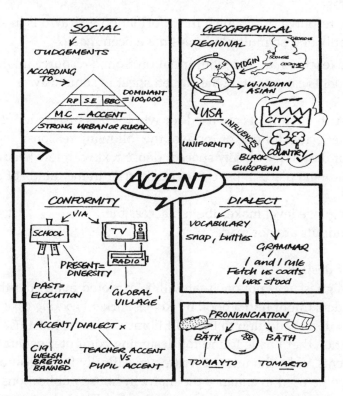

This example is taken, like Example 5, from Strategies for Studying, a superb book on study skills for post-16 students. My thanks to Carel Press for permission to reproduce this here.

5 Using Handouts

The term *'handout'* is used to describe documents that either contain information or tasks. In this chapter on whole-class teaching I am not concerned with the use of handouts that contain instructions, questions or tasks - such handouts are known more commonly as worksheets. This section will examine the use of documents for the presentation of information, textual, numerical or visual, which are used by teachers as a stimulus or as a resource to support whole-class instruction. Teachers produce such documents for a variety of reasons:

- The information has been compiled by the teacher from a variety of sources and has been copied to provide access to whole classes.

- The resource from which the information is drawn is in short supply and so multiple copies have been made.

- The teacher has copied information from a resource in order that students can annotate the copied sheet in some way.

When such documents are used for whole-class instruction they are often ineffective for one or more of the following reasons:
(a) Poor design (eg closely spaced, dense text with few headings or sub-headings) places a psychological barrier in the minds of the students.
(b) Language level makes them inaccessible.
(c) Handouts are not read.

(a) Poor design
The design issue is not one that will be explored in any depth here but readers might find a book by Roger Parker, '*Looking Good in Print*', a useful addition to the staff library. It is the most useful publication that I have found for designing computer generated documents and although not written specifically for education, the book can be used to enhance the many in-house publications that schools produce for their various audiences. The book is so useful because it not only explains the theory of good design but illustrates it with concrete examples. The page from the book that is reproduced below examines the use of white space in design.

Use of White Space   Example 8

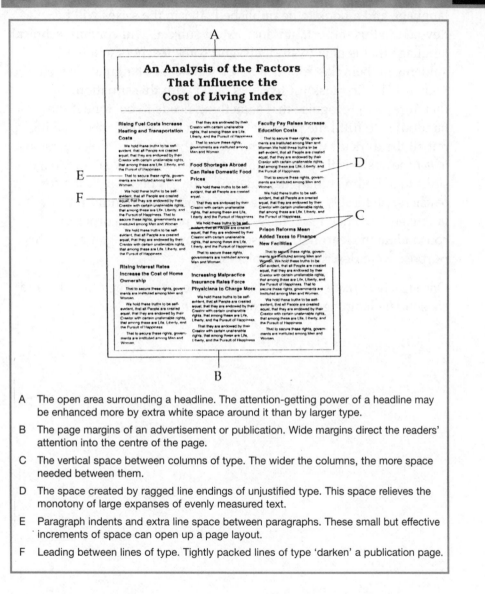

A   The open area surrounding a headline. The attention-getting power of a headline may be enhanced more by extra white space around it than by larger type.

B   The page margins of an advertisement or publication. Wide margins direct the readers' attention into the centre of the page.

C   The vertical space between columns of type. The wider the columns, the more space needed between them.

D   The space created by ragged line endings of unjustified type. This space relieves the monotony of large expanses of evenly measured text.

E   Paragraph indents and extra line space between paragraphs. These small but effective increments of space can open up a page layout.

F   Leading between lines of type. Tightly packed lines of type 'darken' a publication page.

My thanks to Ventana Communications (a Thompson Company) for permission to use this extract.

● ● ● ● ●

(b) Language level

I have emphasised before the need for teachers at all levels to build language and a book to be published later in the series will be devoted to this important issue. Most subjects will contain technical language that is new to students, and some teachers will have students in their classrooms whose weakness in language is well-known. The first task for teachers faced with this situation, therefore, is to recognise that something needs to be done if the handout is to fulfil the purpose for which it was designed. Taking out all the difficult words and replacing them with simpler versions is *not* the answer; that will condemn students with weak language skills to a lifetime of language deprivation. A better solution for teachers, preferably as part of a team effort, is to identify the key language, and then teach it, re-visiting it regularly in order to consolidate the learning; the use of display and card games for this purpose were described in Book One.

Once teachers have adopted this principle, the strategy to build and consolidate language can be extended to handouts.

Identify Key Language   Example 9

The display of key language (buzz words) at the top of each handout or activity sheet prepares students for the new vocabulary and as a result fewer students will struggle when confronted with unfamiliar language. This example is from a Home Economics booklet on Healthy Eating.

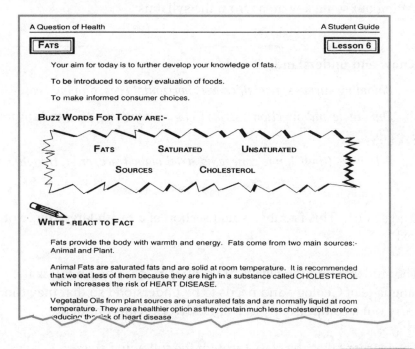

My thanks to the Home Economics Department of Forres Academy, near Inverness, for permission to reproduce this here.

● ● ● ● ●

In Chapter Three of Book One I argued strongly that teachers should share assessment criteria with their students. Some teachers have done this in the past simply by photocopying the appropriate sections from the syllabus. This is not always very helpful because many examination boards produce syllabus information in a language that is alien to most teachers, let alone students. Attempts must be made, therefore, to make sense of such information if it is to be of any use to the students.

Example 10   # Making Sense of Jargon

In this example a teacher of A Level Geology has come up with an ingenious approach to teaching an area of the syllabus that students in his experience find extremely challenging.

The extract below comes from a handout prepared by the teacher setting out some key areas from the syllabus:

Know and understand

Bounding surfaces, true thickness, horizontal beds, dipping beds.

Dip (angle and direction), strike (3 figure azimuth), true and apparent dip.

Fold parts (limb, hinge zone, axis, axial plane trace, crest, trough).

And so on... This is only a small section of a much larger piece of text.

The students find the technical vocabulary daunting but it is the language of Geology and needs to be understood so that they can carry out a compulsory piece of fieldwork with confidence.

The teacher takes the class through the following stages:

Stage 1 Looking at the handout they agree it is mostly 'jargon'.

Stage 2 The teacher uses textbooks, slides, videos and maps to examine some concrete examples of structural geology.

Stage 3 The students are told that they will have to undertake a field course for coursework where they will have to know, understand and apply (a) the jargon and (b) the necessary skills.

Stage 4 In order to complete the field course with confidence the students are now required to design a *field guide* for structural geology.

Stage 5 The class discuss with each other and the teacher what should be in this guide and how it should be presented.

Stage 6 Small groups of students each prepare their own field guide making sense of jargon in the process.

Stage 7 Each group constructs a structural feature using chicken wire and foam.

Stage 8 The teacher shows the whole class how to make field notes from their structure, explaining

> how/what to observe,
>
> how/what to measure (including what equipment to use),
>
> how/what to record.

Stage 9 The students in their groups then make field notes based on the model their group constructed. All models are then destroyed.

Stage 10 The field notes are then self-assessed by each student using à form provided by the teacher and then handed to another group which has to use them to construct another group's original model.

Stage 11 The second group then assesses the field notes they were given to use.

Stage 12 The teacher tests the whole class on the jargon.

Stage 13 The students undertake the actual fieldwork.

This is a good example of how to use an active class teaching approach to help students acquire, interpret and use technical language originally introduced on a handout. Its strength is that it requires students to turn technical language into a field guide for others to use. Producing a product for an audience, as I pointed out in Book One, never fails to raise the motivation of students, to improve the quality of the eventual product (the field guide), and to deepen understanding. When the concepts are used for real in the coursework later, students will be familiar with the jargon and will be able to plan coursework in line with the criteria.

My thanks to Richard Pepper, Head of Science at St Mary RC Sixth Form College, Middlesbrough, for permission to use this here.

● ● ● ● ●

(c) Handouts are not read

Most teachers will be familiar with the students who judge their work effort on the weight of the handouts they have managed to collect. This situation is more common with students in the sixth form but it can happen with younger students, particularly with those who are lazy or those who have low self-esteem or little confidence; a two kilo folder is a wonderful way to convince parents that you are working hard.   Teachers who distribute handouts must, therefore, find a way of ensuring that students engage with the information or data and make sense of it.

Example 11   Concept Mapping

Stage 1 Students are given an envelope containing key words (concepts) on pieces of card.

Stage 2 Students in groups of about three are given an A3 sheet and asked to lay out the key words and to connect them with arrows. Students must write a note of explanation on each arrow.

Stage 3 The teacher brings the class together and in turn the groups explain their diagrams, justify the links they have made and answer questions from other students or the teacher.

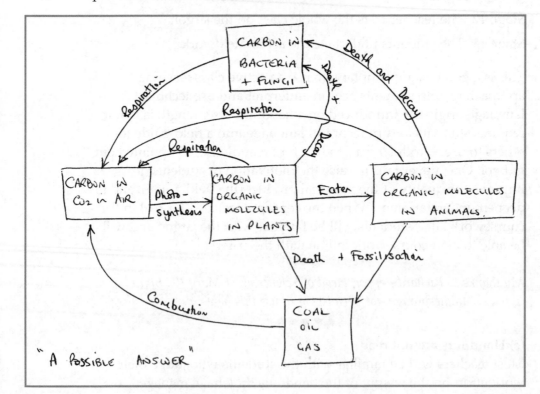

This particular activity was used by the teacher with a group of GCSE students after lessons on the carbon cycle, and with an A Level Biology group before teaching nutrient cycles. The idea could be used by any teacher where conceptual links need to be made.

It has a number of learning benefits:

➡ It requires students to make sense of notes or information from a text book.
➡ It provides students with a visual representation which, for some, will aid both understanding and memory.
➡ It helps the teacher check understanding.
➡ It encourages discussion, analysis and peer coaching.
➡ Motivation is enhanced because of the product/audience nature of the activity.

My thanks to Peter Richards, Teaching and Learning Coordinator at Morriston Comprehensive School in Swansea for sending in this example. He has based the idea on the work of Richard White and Richard Gunstone, authors of 'Probing Understanding', published by Falmer Press.

Summarising Notes for Others   Example 12

In this example the teacher has divided the notes into four sections and printed them on four separate handouts. The class is divided into a number of small groups and each group is given only one of the handouts. (For large classes, more than one group can work on the same handout.) Each group is then given the task of completing a summary sheet, possibly for homework or in private study, which will then be presented to the rest of the class in a plenary. The teacher will compile a final version of each handout on the blackboard or OHP, intervening, of course, to correct mistakes or to point out omissions. The completed versions of each handout are then written up by students.This approach has a number of learning benefits:

➡ Students have to process the notes in the handouts, make sense of them and produce the key information in a different form. This cannot be done without understanding.

➡ Teaching others is one of the best ways to deepen understanding

➡ Small groups have to collaborate and in doing so peer coaching is likely.

• • • • •

The close reading of information is a skill that is needed in most courses and at most levels. Most teachers at some point in their own teaching will ask students to read a section from a textbook, an article from a newspaper or magazine, or a handout containing important information or data. The success or otherwise of the activity is dependent not only on whether students can understand or interpret the language but on whether they have the inner motivation to 'plough through' what is to them a mass of meaningless or 'boring' text. Some teachers have devised ingenious ways to make the task more interesting.

Example 13	Producing Evidence Cards

Students are asked to read through the document (handout, textbook, article etc) that forms the basis for the lesson. Once the students have finished the reading they have to work in pairs to identify five or six important key points, facts or data from the text. Each pair must then record onto postcard sized pieces of paper, clues to the facts that they have chosen, being careful not to give the answer away by making the clues too obvious. These *'evidence cards'* as the pieces of paper are called, form the basis of the whole-class plenary, where each pair of students reads out one of their clues for others to solve. The more clues they have to read out the more subtle the clue.

This technique works well for the following reasons:

➡ It can be used with most age groups and in most subjects with little preparation.

➡ Reading is done with a real purpose and with a product (evidence cards) in mind.

➡ In order to work out a clue students have to make sense of the text.

➡ The desire to set a problem that others can't solve leads to students working out subtle clues, ones that challenge both the students setting the problem and the ones who desperately want to solve it.

➡ Students enjoy it.

6 Clarity and understanding

Teachers may have followed all the advice so far offered in this chapter and many students will have benefited from the strategies adopted. Some, however, will still be unable to access or interpret the information, data or skills that have been introduced. Teachers who recognise that students are unlikely to respond honestly to the 'is everyone clear?' question will therefore have to find a strategy to help those who still have gaps in their understanding. One of the best strategies that I have come across for providing support to such students is through the use of support groups, the concept which was introduced as Ground Rule 8 in Chapter One.

Using Support Groups to Aid Clarity   Example 1

The teacher has distributed a copy of a handout on Roman Britain to each student and has taken the class through it, using visuals and concrete examples to illustrate the content. At regular intervals the teacher stops and directs the students to join other members of their support group. Each time they do this the group has two tasks to perform:

1 Are all members of the group clear about what has been covered so far? If any individual is uncertain about anything - language, content, interpretation - then others in the group who do understand must try to explain.

2 If there is something that all members of the group are finding difficult then the chairperson (Ground Rule 3) must ask for support from the teacher. This approach to the 'is everyone clear?' question provides an opportunity for students to develop clarity, confidence and understanding in an environment that is fundamentally 'safe':

➡ No-one has to own up publicly.

➡ Students help each other rather than being totally dependent on the teacher.

➡ Requests for help come through the anonymity of the chairperson.

➡ Fewer students proceed to the next phase with problems of understanding.

Furthermore, this approach means that teachers can maintain the concentration of students by moving regularly from whole-class instruction to short bursts of participation, including discussion, questioning and interpretation.

This use of support groups can be productive with classes of all ages and in all subjects. Its success depends partly on the ground rules that were explained in Chapter One and on the care and sensitivity that is shown by teachers in the selection of groups.

If teachers use the support group approach they will bring into the open misunderstandings or lack of clarity that would otherwise remain undetected until later - *'I couldn't do the homework because I didn't understand...'* There is no guarantee, however, that students will always remember something that has been explained by either the support group or the teacher. It is a good idea, therefore, for teachers to find a way for students to make notes on the topic/concept/language that has just been explained. The design of handouts is one way to do this.

Example 15	Using White Space for Clarifying

The handout in this example sets out for students important information related to an assignment that they will have to complete as one of their pieces of coursework. The teacher is using the handout as an information sheet clarifying important points concerning deadlines, criteria, presentation and so on. It is very important that students leave this lesson absolutely clear about what is required because the teacher has asked them to prepare, for homework, an outline plan of their proposed study. The teacher, using whole-class teaching interspersed with periods of discussion in support groups, is taking students through the information sheet.

The major difference between this example and Example 14 is that
when students have had certain points clarified they add notes in
the wide margin of the handout.

The wide margin is one
approach, another is the one
below where space has been left
between paragraphs or sections.

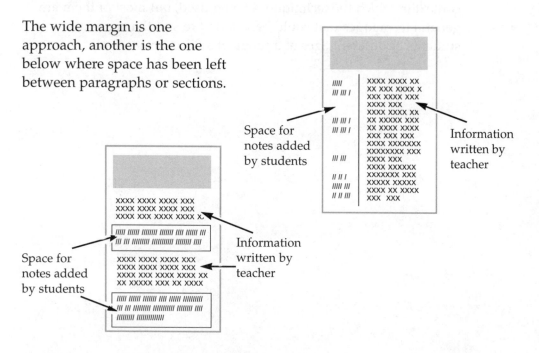

Space for
notes added
by students

Information
written by
teacher

Space for
notes added
by students

Information
written by
teacher

Such a design has a number of points to commend it:

➡ Notes made *by* students are more likely to make sense than ones
   made *for* them.

➡ Students only add notes where they are needed and so each
   handout becomes personalised. Students can make notes in a
   style that suits them (eg graphics, abbreviations, concrete
   examples etc).

➡ The students have a visual reminder because the notes are part
   of the document that they will use in the planning of the
   coursework.

The big drawback in the eyes of some teachers, however, is that the
handout cannot now be used again by other students - it has become
a consumable. Teachers will have to make professional judgments in
weighing up the benefits against the costs.

● ● ● ● ●

This chapter has concentrated on techniques that can be used in whole-class instruction. The examples used identify the particular context in which the technique is being used, but most of them are general techniques that could be adapted to suit the needs of students of different ages in a range of subject areas.

Chapter Three

Whole-Class Teaching for Questioning and Thinking

This chapter will examine:

- Ground rules for questioning and thinking

- Questioning techniques

- Thinking techniques

Whole-Class Teaching for Questioning and Thinking

Readers may have heard the story of the inspector for Mathematics who was observing a teacher practising mental arithmetic with a class in a question/answer session. Every time the teacher posed a question all the hands shot in the air. The inspector was very impressed and graded the lesson highly. Keen to praise the students, she said to one student as they met in the doorway on the way out:

> *'Well done, you did well there.'*
> *'No I didn't'*, replied the student, *'I found it hard.'*
> *'You seemed keen to put your hand up,'* said the inspector, a little perplexed.
> *'No'*, answered the student quickly, *'you don't understand. I was putting up my left hand. The teacher told us to use our right hands if we knew the answer and our left hands if we didn't!'*

This teacher found a way to encourage participation in a whole-class question and answer session and whilst teachers would be unwise to follow this example, it does illustrate the frustration some colleagues feel when confronted with classes of passive students.

Question/answer sessions that actively involve only a few students cannot be considered effective and yet the approach is widely used. This chapter, therefore, will examine techniques that can be adopted when teachers are using whole-class questioning in order to test immediate understanding, to aid interpretation or to develop thinking skills. All the techniques will emphasise the need to increase participation, to raise motivation, and, as ever, to aid deeper understanding and long-term learning.

I emphasised in Chapter One that good whole-class teaching relies to a large degree on a set of clearly defined ground rules. Some of these will apply in whole-class questioning, and two, in particular, are worth repeating here:

Ground Rule 1 All contributions are valued and no put-downs, abuse or ridicule are allowed.

Ground Rule 2 All contributions go through the chair (teacher or student).

There are other strategies, however, that teachers would do well to consider if such sessions are to be really effective.

1 Make eye contact with students.

2 Make sure that your voice is non-threatening and your body language relaxed - this is a learning situation not a confrontation.

3 Try to grab the attention of students from the beginning: pose a problem, present them with a mystery to solve, pretend that you are confused and need help (you may be!).

4 Start with simple questions and increase the challenge gradually. Start from the familiar and move into the abstract.

5 Avoid questions that can be answered by a simple *'yes'* or *'no'*. Questions that involve *'why'*, *'how'*, *'when'*, *'who'* or *'what would happen if...'* are more likely to lead to thoughtful responses.

6 Avoid the *'guess what answer I want'* approach - all students do is make as many guesses as possible and teachers ignore valuable contributions in their quest for the *'right'* answer.

7 Ask the question before naming the student - everyone will be listening; if you name the student first only one may be listening.

8 Do not butt in too quickly if there is a silence - students soon learn that if they say nothing the teacher will answer for them.

9 Develop the skills of listening; make sure that you listen carefully to students' contributions and check that students are listening to each other.

10 Stop the questioning at regular intervals for a short period of consolidation and review.

These strategies will be no more than good practice for the successful whole-class teacher. Some teachers, of course, who make regular use of whole-class teaching, will not see the need to use such techniques because they have motivated, articulate or confident students, or because they teach an age group which is naturally inquisitive and enthusiastic. Many teachers, however, do not enjoy such advantages and for them the guidance set out above will not be sufficient to make their whole-class teaching effective:

- Do not butt in too quickly sounds a sensible idea but some classes are thicker-skinned than the teacher and will happily sit in silence until the teacher's resolve breaks.

- Teachers may want to adopt a non-threatening manner but that is not easy in some classes where behaviour is a problem.

- Grabbing their interest with a mystery or problem to solve is a good idea in theory but in some classes only two respond.

- Ask open-ended questions like *'Why did Hitler start the Second World War?'*. Such advice is in the teachers' manual, but nowhere does it tell you what to do when the student replies *'To win'*.

The reality for many teachers is that question/answer sessions with whole-classes are not always easy and that is why some teachers resort to a worksheet approach where the students can at least appear to be engaged in a task.

The techniques that follow will not necessarily produce the panacea that all teachers crave - there are few instant solutions in education as the previous government with its *'one new idea a week'* philosophy found to its own cost. But I can reassure colleagues brave enough to try something new that the techniques work and they are fun!

I can see the letters' page of some national newspapers now:

> *'Dear Sir, When are we going to rid ourselves of these trendy educationalists with their progressive 60s' ideas? When I was at school I was not there to enjoy myself. I was beaten every day and hated every minute, but it never did me any harm...'*

The purpose of these techniques is not to have fun; it is to develop motivation, understanding and to raise levels of achievement. If the techniques also increase the enjoyment levels of both students and teachers then that is merely a bonus. But never let anyone make you feel guilty about using approaches that, for example, make students laugh. The chances are that the experience will remain with them and, when required to recall facts or information in examinations, they will remember...

Participation in Questioning

Once students have passed beyond the 'MeMe' phase described in the introduction, many choose not to participate and teachers resort to the 'volunteer' and 'conscript' approach.   The technique that is examined in the following example can be used with all age groups and with all subjects, indeed it works well with teachers on in-service training. It is being used here to encourage students to ask questions.   In many classrooms the only questions asked are those put by the teacher and where this happens students learn to be passive. The whole process of whole-class questioning is enhanced if students are encouraged to ask thoughtful questions as well as respond to those put by the teacher.

The Snowball Technique - Generating Questions   Example 16

The History teacher with a group of A Level or Highers students has asked them to read a handout or a chapter in the text book. When they have all finished, instead of saying 'any questions?', which she knows will result in the mass shaking of heads, she uses the snowball technique.

Stage 1 All students, working on their own, are asked to make a note of any section, vocabulary, event or concept that they would like explained further. The time scale for this stage will depend on the length of the text.

Stage 2 In pairs they exchange their chosen problems, helping each other to solve them if possible.

Stage 3 In small groups they pool the problems defined by each pair and offer help to each other if one of the students is confident enough to do so.

Stage 4 The teacher draws the class together and takes one question or problem from each group in turn. (Ground Rule 10 on page 19 would work well here where each group has a Chair and a Scribe.) Some teachers will take the questions that come from one group and re-direct them to the remaining groups before replying themselves thus reinforcing the participation.

The snowball technique used in this context has a number of learning benefits:

➡ Shy students are able to have their queries answered in a 'safe' environment without the fear of ridicule or embarrassment.

➡ The process involves dialogue between students which can help to develop confidence and understanding.

➡ Students are sometimes reluctant to seek clarification because they think all the others students understand. The use of the snowball in this way will expose this myth and give students greater confidence in seeking help.

➡ The process of moving from the individual to the pair to the group makes it far more difficult for individuals to opt out, leaving others to do the work, or for groups to be dominated by assertive students who take over and ignore the contributions of others. If the scribe uses initials, as described in Ground Rule 11, then full participation is almost certainly assured.

➡ More students will receive praise for their contributions than would be the case in the *'hands up'* approach.

➡ Students are encouraged to reflect more carefully on the meaning of the text they are studying.

● ● ● ● ●

Teachers of Mathematics traditionally make great use of question/answer sessions but they are not immune to the passive student syndrome; indeed, regular and public humiliation in an oral mental arithmetic lesson can create great fear in students, leaving them with a phobia of mathematics for the rest of their lives. The three examples that follow show how Mathematics can actually be fun!

Start with the Problem   Example 1

Many teachers of Mathematics move through a sequence of teaching, followed by practice and ending with a problem to solve. Sometimes, a degree of excitement can be generated by starting from the problem:

> *If a cow and a goat could eat all the grass in a field in 45 days, and a cow and a goose could eat all the grass in the same field in 60 days, and a goat and a goose could eat the same amount in 90 days, how long would it take the goat, cow and goose to eat the grass when put into the field together?*

Proportional reasoning is one of the sticking points in many people's repertoire of arithmetic skills. Fractions, ratios and relationships between proportional increase and decrease leave many of us stumped. Starting a lesson with a problem, and encouraging groups to pool their ideas can create a climate for productive, whole-class discussion and learning.

Another successful starting point, and one which reveals students' knowledge and skills in number, is presented thus:

> *You have some positive numbers whose sum is 17; what is the highest product you can make?*

Most students start with pairs of integers and then move on to triples etc. As the lesson progresses, particularly successful combinations will become evident. Those with confidence will progress into decimal numbers. Working in pairs and using the snowball technique is also very effective.

Mathematics is often seen as a subject where the teacher presents the question and students find the answer. With younger students productive and enjoyable lessons can start with the teacher writing on the blackboard:

The answer is 11.

Faced with this problem students can show creativity and ingenuity and a degree of understanding and skill often beyond the expectation of the teacher. Valuable teaching points can emerge through this activity as the following response of a seven-year-old to the problem demonstrates:

$2 + 9 =$	$2 + 4 + 5 =$	
$1 + 10 =$	$12 - 1 =$	$20 - 9 =$
$1 + 2 + 8 =$	$1 + 8 + 2 =$	$8 + 2 + 1 =$
$11 + 0 =$	$6 + 5 =$	$13 - 2 =$
$10 + 1 =$	$5 + 6 =$	$14 - 3 =$
$9 + 2 =$	$4 + 7 =$	$15 - 4 =$
$1 + 10 =$	$3 + 8 =$	$16 - 5 =$
$10 + 1 =$	$2 + 9 =$	$17 - 6 =$
$9 + 2 =$	$1 + 10 =$	$18 - 7 =$
$8 + 3 =$	$0 + 11 =$	$19 - 8 =$
$7 + 4 =$	$12 - 1 =$	$20 - 9 =$
$21 - 10 =$		

This student worked through the numbers in an orderly way up to 11. The 12 - 1 example suggests that he may be beginning to get into the concept of negative numbers and this type of response is a good opening for dialogue '...why did you...?'

My thanks to Peter Lacey, Senior Adviser for North East Lincolnshire, for providing me with these examples.

● ● ● ● ●

Kinesthetic Mathematics   Example 18

Kinesthetic intelligence is one of the seven intelligences described earlier. It is concerned with movement or making and its use in this example is in Mathematics. The teacher has instructed a class of ten-year-olds on the rules concerning the decimal point and the students have completed a short series of exercises from the work book. The teacher now brings a number of students out to sit on chairs at the front of the class and places a piece of card around each of their necks, each one with a digit on it. One of the students has a piece of card with a decimal point printed on it and she is placed by the teacher somewhere in the line.

When they are lined up a number is displayed. For example:

5 4 3 9 7 8 6 . 9 0

The teacher then calls out a series of calculations:

'Divide by 100.'

'Divide by a 1000.'

'Multiply by 10.'

The student with the decimal point has to remain seated and the others have to move up or down the line to the correct place each time the teacher calls out, with the rest of the class deciding whether the positions chosen by the students are correct or not. The teacher can do this as many times as felt necessary, changing the numbers or the students to vary the challenge and give everyone a chance of participating. Students can also be encouraged to shout out a calculation but if this happens they must tell the rest of the class whether the response of the students at the front is correct or not. Another alternative is for the students at the front to make their own decisions about movement and the rest of the class have to work out what the calculation was.

Example 19   **Bingo**

Each student is given a bingo card with the usual range of numbers displayed. The teacher calls out a calculation for example 3 x 7. All students who have 21 on their bingo cards can cover it over with a counter. (The cards can be used again if they are not written on.) Alternatively, the teacher can produce bingo cards which have the calculations on eg 77-12, $64 \div 8$, or 27+6. When the teacher calls out the number 33, students can place a counter over the calculation 27+6 or others such as 3x11, 17+16 or $99 \div 3$. The winner is the student, pair or group that is first to cover all their numbers correctly.

1		32		55	61		90
	13		42			89	
4	21			57			
		26	39		62		

Example 20   **Snap**

This game is adapted from the popular card game and is played to similar rules. The teacher prepares sets of cards which have a range of mathematical or arithmetic calculations printed on them. Eg 5x4 or 5.5x10 or 3+7+4-7. The calculations can be as simple or as complex as the teacher chooses.

In groups of about four, students play the game where one student places a card on the table and all do a quick mental calculation. The next student places another card and if this card has an answer that matches the previous one then the word 'snap' is called out.

An alternative is for students to be dealt a range of cards with different numbers on. The first student places one on the table and the students who follow can only lay a card down if they can establish a link:

- they are both primary numbers
- they are both divisible by...
- they ascend in sequence eg x+2, x+4, x+6 etc.

Answer and pass on...   Example 21

In this game students are issued with one card each on which is written both a question and an answer. The first student reads out the question on the card and if someone has the correct answer on her card she calls out the answer. She then reads out the question on her card and someone who has the correct answer calls it out. He then reads out his question and so on...

Students can be issued with more than one card, of course, so that a second round is possible, but if teachers have planned questions to match answers carefully it is a good idea to colour code the cards so that they can be returned to the correct pack. This game could be played in almost any subject eg definitions in A Level Sociology, Sports Science, Biology etc.

This example was adapted from an original activity in 'Numbers and Measures', published by Philip Allen. My thanks to the authors, Professor Afzal Ahmed and Honor Williams of The Chichester Institute of Higher Education.

These approaches to mental arithmetic have a number of learning benefits:

➡ Those who have used kinesthetic approaches argue that students not only enjoy the physical activity but more importantly they remember because they physically performed or observed the application of mathematics.

➡ The degree of challenge can easily be adapted to suit both the skills, confidence and age group of the students.

➡ Older students can develop their own sets of playing cards for younger groups to use, reinforcing their own knowledge and skills and providing stimulus for others.

➡ Students and teachers enjoy it and enjoying arithmetic is one stage in becoming confident with number.

➡ The lesson has pace as students have to concentrate and think quickly.

➡ The game can be integrated with formal instruction or with text book work and in this way motivation and stimulation are ensured.

➡ Card games can be sent home for use as homework, possibly developing numeracy within the family.

The use of games like this is not new - many teachers will introduce such approaches at Christmas or at the end of the term as 'light relief'. Many, however, will see the primary function of games as amusement and will be cautious of using them in 'normal' lessons. This is a shame because they are a very powerful learning tool and can be extremely rigorous and challenging. The examples that follow are also 'games' in the strict sense of the word but if learning is the chief criteria then they can be classified as effective whole-class teaching techniques.

Example 22	Nomination

This game is based on the popular television quiz show '15 to 1' and can be used with any age group, any ability range and within any subject. In this example it is being used to develop language and understanding in a Food Technology department where key vocabulary has been introduced and students are now being tested.

The teacher asks all students to stand up and each in turn is asked to spell a word read out by the teacher. All students have two 'lives' and the names of students who make a mistake are recorded on the blackboard. Students who make a mistake in each of the first two rounds have to sit down and are out of the game.

In round three, which has gone onto meaning, the teacher reads out a word and the student has to both spell it correctly and answer a second question related to meaning. If the student is correct he can nominate who is asked the next question. If the student who is nominated is also correct she can nominate the next, and so on... If however, she answers incorrectly then the student who nominated her can nominate someone else.

This game is extremely popular and is in effect a question/answer session where students participate willingly. The game has a number of learning benefits:

➡ Students and teachers enjoy it.

➡ Differentiation is easy because the teacher can prepare a range of questions with varying degrees of challenge and can choose the difficulty level according to the person being asked.

➡ Because students nominate each other there is a natural desire to learn the topic thoroughly so that friends can't catch you out.

➡ It develops both language and understanding.

➡ It develops speaking and listening skills.

Language and Knowledge Game   Example 23

This game is based on the television quiz 'Blockbusters' and I first came across it being used by a teacher of History in Scotland. He had constructed the overhead below and had devised a range of questions such as:

Green Team

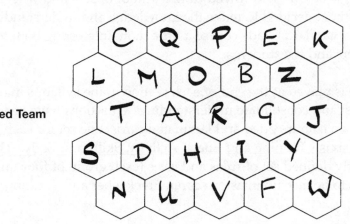

Red Team

Which 'S' is the city where Franz Ferdinand was shot?

Which 'D' was invented by John Fisher in 1904?

Students, playing in two teams, have to try to be first to connect left to right or top to bottom by getting all the appropriate answers right. Teams try to block each other by selecting letters which force the other team to move around. For example, if the Green team has won letters 'T', 'A' and 'R' then the Red team needs to win 'G', then 'B' and then 'I' in order to force the green team to go the long way round to get to the other side. This game has much to commend it:

- ➡ Students and teachers enjoy it.
- ➡ The questions can be made as simple or as challenging as required. (In the example I saw the teacher had up to six alternative questions for each letter.)
- ➡ It can be used for building language.
- ➡ Students can develop their own games for use with the rest of the class.

Example 24	Question of Sport

The television programme by the same name is very popular and few staff or students will not have watched it at one time or another. The example below is borrowed from a school in Scotland where the PE department decided to make the knowledge and understanding side of the Standard Grade course a little more interesting both for the teachers and the students.

The game is played at the end of each section in the syllabus in order both to test and consolidate understanding. Questions have been produced on colour-coded and laminated cards, one set for each area of the syllabus - Training and Effect, Activity, Skills and Body. There are a clearly defined set of rules and roles (each group of four takes it in turns to be questionmaster, scorer, timekeeper and question selector).

A Question of Sport

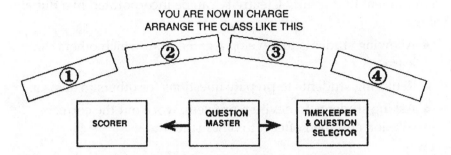

Face the teams - make sure each team is separate from the others.

Ask each team to a) give their team a name b) name a spokesperson.

Bring the competition to order and make sure the rules are clear to everyone.

Ask the question selector on your right what topic is required by selecting a topic card.

Ask the question.

Give time to answer (30 secs) and only accept the answer from the spokesperson.

Decide if the question is answered correctly and award a point - scorer marks score-sheet.

Next question.

Remember there are many answers to some of the questions - the answers given are only a suggestion, so you will have to use your own Knowledge and Understanding to sort out any difficulties.

As a last resort your teacher will help you out.

The questions have been made up by the PE teachers, past students, and taken from past papers.

The PE Department staff cite a number of benefits to their approach:

➡ Students are more motivated than before in the knowledge and understanding lessons.

➡ They are able to recall key information more readily in tests.

➡ Key skills such as speaking clearly, thinking quickly, acting fairly and recording accurately are being developed alongside the PE curriculum.

My thanks to the PE Department from Forres Academy, near Inverness, for permission to use this example.

Once teachers start to use the creativity of students, motivation increases and some colleagues will be startled at the quality and commitment that result. Creativity can be incorporated in a number of ways:

- Allowing students to develop a game from which others can learn.

- Requiring students to prepare questions for others to answer.

- Asking students to devise a problem, work out the correct solution and then offer it to other students.

The examples that follow illustrate ways in which this can be done.

Example 25   **Snakes and Ladders**

In this example a teacher of History has introduced a class of eleven-year-olds to the topic *The Church in the Middle Ages*. They have been through a number of formal lessons involving instruction, reading and discussion, and a short period of small group research. The topic ends with each small group of students having to devise a game of snakes and ladders based on the theme 'Heaven and Hell'. They have to design the board, illustrate it - some homework is involved - and then prepare questions on the subject matter of the topic which will be displayed at key points. For example:

Name the place between Heaven and Hell (Purgatory).

Give two reasons why someone might go on a pilgrimage (Penance or Healing).

Explain what a Tithe is (one tenth of all income given to the church).

As in the normal game of snakes and ladders students have to reach the top *(Heaven)* but if they make mistakes they might drop to the bottom *(Hell)*. The teacher explains that whether students go up or down depends upon the quality of the questions and that each group would be assessed on (a) the quality and accuracy of their questions, (b) the use and understanding of key language (eg *purgatory*), (c) presentation of the board and (d) the degree of enjoyment in playing the game. Each game that is produced is played by other groups and at the end this particular teacher asked the Head of Department to judge what had been achieved.

My thanks to Anthony Kemp from the History Department at St John Fisher RC Comprehensive School in Chatham, Kent, for permission to use this idea.

Hangman   Example 26

This game can be played individually although in a large class it will probably work better in pairs. The example is drawn from Modern Languages but the idea will work in most subjects. Students are asked to learn or revise vocabulary on a particular topic and then prepare a series of questions for the rest of the class. There are a number of ways in which this might be done:

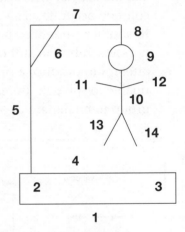

- they hold up a photograph (eg an apple)

- they point to a part of the body (eg the head)

- they mime an action (eg eating)

- they hold up a word in the target language (eg une assiette)

After each pair has asked its question students swop books and mark the answer immediately. All the pairs that have the correct answer can add a stroke of the pen to their hangman diagram. As the illustration shows, it takes fourteen correct answers to finish the drawing and the winners will be first to do so. The students who win will be those who can answer all the questions put by others in the class but are able to ask a question that no-one else can do.

Example 27

Pass the Problem

This example is drawn from Mathematics but might be used in other areas where problem-solving is used eg Science or Technology.

The teacher has been teaching the concept of area to a group of ten-year-olds and the class has experienced whole-class teaching and individual work using text book exercises. Students are then asked to devise a problem where the solution can be obtained by applying what has been learned in the earlier lessons. All students or pairs of students (teacher choice) are told that they must not only devise a problem but also work out the correct solution on a separate sheet of paper, showing the workings. Once they have finished they must call the teacher who will check that the problem is fair and the solution accurate. The teacher then takes the problem and hands it to another student or pair who are asked to solve it. Their response is assessed by the authors. The example below is an obvious attempt to produce a problem so complicated that others will be unable to solve it. In reality, of course, it merely fires up the other group to retaliate.

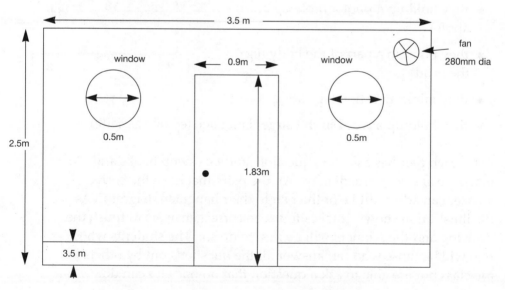

How many square metres of wallpaper are needed for this wall?

The last three examples share many of the characteristics of earlier approaches:

➡ They encourage participation.

➡ They develop quick-thinking.

➡ They are enjoyable.

➡ They aid longer-term memory.

But these also have a number of other key features:

➡ They involve creative thinking.

➡ They involve the production of a product.

➡ They demand that students ask as well as answer questions.

This last point is very important. In order to ask a question of someone else the rules state that students have to know the answer. Most students love to ask questions that their peers cannot answer - they go for the *jugular* - and so in the process of forming questions, students go to the limits of their own understanding or skill. This type of approach is therefore excellent for developing challenge within the classroom and can also be used in developing revision strategies, examples of which will be described in Chapter Four.

Whole-Class Teaching and Thinking Skills

Question/answer sessions with whole-class groups are also used to develop thinking skills. The reason why this is necessary is aptly summed up by this story from inspection.

A junior school teacher of Science was investigating the concept of friction with a class of ten-year-olds. She had ingeniously brought into school a large, heavy-duty box, had attached a rope to one of the handles and had asked one of the class to sit in the box while members of the class pulled it around the school. The purpose of this activity was to investigate the degree of friction in different kinds of surface - carpet, concrete, wood block or ceramic tile. The Science Inspector walked around with the children, making notes on his clip board. At one point he stopped the children:

'How could we make this test a bit fairer?' he asked in an inquisitive tone.
'We all get a go in the box,' was the instant reply.

Skilful questioning by teachers is very important but time must also be spent on developing the students ability to think. This story illustrates the difficulty some teachers have in encouraging students to move beyond the low-level response. Some examples of how some teachers have tackled this issue are therefore included in this chapter.

Example 28   **The Snowball Technique - Generating Ideas**

The teacher has been talking to the class about life in the times of the Vikings. He wants to encourage the students to think about the living conditions faced by ordinary people in those times and instead of asking for suggestions through a 'hands up' approach he uses the 'snowball' technique.

Stage 1 All students are given one minute in silence to think of one problem faced by people living in Viking times. They are told to record their ideas on a piece of rough paper. The teacher patrols the class during that one minute exercise offering quiet praise and encouragement.

Stage 2 The teacher now instructs the class to work for two minutes in pairs, exchanging their original ideas with their partner, and then to think of a third idea between them. The teacher continues to patrol and praise the ideas that are emerging. After three or four minutes all pairs should have at least three ideas.

Stage 3 The students are now asked to form themselves into groups of four made up of two existing pairs (it might be a support group). Each pair must exchange their ideas and then as a group think of two new ideas. The teacher, once again, patrols the room offering praise. This exercise might last for three or four minutes.

Stage 4 The teacher draws the class back together and leads a plenary session where the ideas from each of the groups are collated onto the blackboard or onto an OHT. During the plenary the teacher takes one idea only from each group in turn. This is important because if he were to invite one group to read out its entire list other groups would groan in disappointment saying '..*we had that'*.

The technique used in this way offers a number of learning benefits:

➡ Students who are normally too shy to volunteer have an opportunity to contribute their ideas.

➡ All students participate throughout the exercise and not just the confident few as would be the case in the 'hands up' approach.

➡ The discussion between students involves learning - negotiating, explaining, questioning will all take place at some time in the snowball process.

➡ Some teachers would go straight into groups from stage 1. But moving from the individual to the pair to the group reduces the chances of groups being dominated by one person and also makes it more difficult for three lazy students to leave one person to do all the work.

➡ During stages 1-3 the teacher is able to patrol the room keeping an eye on progress. The number of students who receive a word of praise or encouragement is far higher than the three or four that are praised in the 'volunteers and conscripts' approach.

➡ The students are encouraged to think more deeply and if Ground Rule 11 (page 19) is used the teacher can praise the contributor during the exercise.

● ● ● ● ●

The snowball technique was seen here being used by a junior school teacher on the subject of Vikings but could be used for generating ideas or developing thinking skills with any age group in any subject or topic. The technique has much to commend it but it may still lead to unimaginative responses unless specific attempts have been made by teachers to train students to think more deeply. Too many whole-class question/answer sessions involve low-level responses where the teacher has a specific answer in mind and the keen students desperately try to guess what it is. Alternative solutions or ideas are rejected and if this happens too often students become conditioned to the 'right answer' syndrome, where, if they are not certain that their contribution is the 'correct' one, they play safe and decide not to speak. Teachers must, therefore, encourage students to think deeply, to offer tentative solutions and to be adventurous; the confidence to do this will come if there is regular practice on topics which are open-ended and where various interpretations and solutions are possible.

Example 29	Cort Thinking

As a young teacher I used to use with my younger classes the *Edward De Bono Cort Thinking Skills* course, and one of the activities was known as PMI (Plus, Minus, Interesting). Students were given a statement such as *'All cars should be painted yellow'*.   The idea sounds at first to be ridiculous but in short bursts of group work students are required to list reasons why this might be a good idea (P), reasons why it is not a good idea (M) and reasons that are merely interesting (I). It was remarkable how many students were motivated by the challenge of coming up with plus points for yellow cars. There were many varied exercises in the course but all were superb for developing the skills of lateral thinking and of good questioning.

The De Bono thinking skills programme is one of a number of published resources on this topic, another being the *Somerset Thinking Skills Course.* But teachers who recognise the need to develop thinking skills, or the ability to ask good, searching questions, do not always need a published resource; they devise their own strategies.   One approach that is successful in encouraging students to think deeply and to pose intelligent questions is to ask them to complete a task where there is insufficient information.

● ● ● ● ●

Thinking - Leaving Information Out

Example 30

In this example students in small groups of four are given a map of an imaginary island called Werehon. Each group must play the role of the island's government in deciding where to build 50km of road, an airport and 30km of railway. They have no further information.

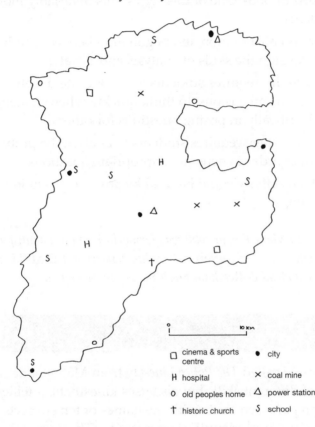

Stage 1 Students spend up to 30 minutes in their groups making decisions and marking their choices on a large copy of the map.

Stage 2 The teacher calls everyone back together and one or more groups present their decisions to the class. Constructive criticism (not abuse) is allowed from the audience.

Stage 3 The teacher asks some searching questions eg *'Why did you build the airport next to the smallest city?'* It becomes clear that no-one can do the exercise properly without much more information than was initially provided.

Stage 4 Each group is required to agree ten questions that they would need answering if they were to do the exercise again (this could be an individual exercise for homework).

This example works well for a number of reasons:

➡ There is both a product and an audience involved and, as I argued in Book One of this series, this invariably motivates students.

➡ There is collaboration and negotiation between students which will develop the skills of analysis and debate.

➡ The activity requires students to think quite deeply in reaching their own conclusions, to think quickly when challenged, and to think critically in posing questions for others.

➡ The final stage requires students to analyse the problem in some depth in order to generate appropriate questions.

➡ Such an activity could be used by any age group in practically any subject.

My thanks to Mark Farrar who was formerly Head of Faculty at Sir John Leman High School in Suffolk, where his department used this idea. He is now Deputy Head of Reetham High School in Norwich.

Example 31	Use the Clues

This example called *The Police Line-Up* from Mathematics develops a number of different skills but also uses kinesthetic intelligence. The teacher prepares ten cards with the names of ten suspects for a police line-up in an identification parade. (The names chosen in this example were boys' names but it would work equally well with girls' names. In the case of a police line-up mixed gender will not work!)

Some of the ten characters were:

Other students in the class (the audience) are given a sheet with a copy of all the clues. The clues on the sheet are:

Bugsy is taller than Spike.

Spike is taller than Mike.

Mugsy is shorter than Mike.

Lefty is taller than Mike, but shorter than Spike.

Fingers is standing somewhere between Benny and Bert.

Bert is shorter than Bugsy, but taller than Fingers.

Frankie is standing between Bugsy and Clyde.

Clyde is next to Bert.

There are seven suspects standing between Frankie and Mugsy.

A witness identifies the fourth (4th) tallest suspect as the criminal.

Who is it?

Stage 1 Members of the audience call out clues randomly and the suspects move up and down the line to their instructions. It soon becomes apparent that this method of solving the problem is chaotic and that a more systematic approach is required. One of the skills of thinking mathematically has already been realised!

Stage 2 The teacher allocates one clue on a card to each of ten students who take it in turns to read out the clue in front of them and the suspects move accordingly. It is important that clue 'owners' check that their clues still apply after a different clue has been acted out. For example, Clyde may be instructed to move so that Frankie is between him and Bugsy, but someone else calls out that Clyde is now no longer next to Bert.

Stage 3 After much negotiation and debate the suspect is named when all the clue owners are satisfied.

This particular exercise can be extended or modified:
- Change one clue
- Students write their own versions
- Work backwards from a solution
- Use different features (eg hairstyles)
- Change the names to numbers. Use for ordering whole/decimal numbers
- Change names to numbers and find the median, mode and calculate the mean. Do all of these people (numbers) exist in the line-up?

This type of activity has a number of benefits:
- It gives practice in logical thinking.
- It develops reading for understanding.
- Students practise communication skills.
- They have to record results accurately.

And, finally, quoting the teacher who sent me this example,

> 'These activities become far more memorable than a diet of textbook questions.'

My thanks to Andy Martin, Head of Mathematics at Thorne Grammar School, near Doncaster. This activity was adapted from the Mathematics Task Centre Project, from Victoria, Australia, who have developed over 100 activities like the Police Line-Up and kindly gave permission for its use in this book.

Robert Powell Publications will publish a book during the Spring of 1998 which contains all the activities from the project that can be used in whole-class teaching with the 11-18 age range. Another book will also be published during the Spring Term setting out a wide range of whole-class teaching activities in Mathematics aimed at the primary age group.

Chapter Four

Whole-Class Teaching for Reviewing, Testing and Revising

This chapter will examine:

■ Reviewing

■ Testing

■ Revising

Whole-Class Teaching for Reviewing, Testing and Revising.

I wonder how many readers teach students who walk into the classroom and say:

> *'Can we have a test today?'*

I am writing this late at night at the end of my first week of headship and you would not be blamed for thinking,

> *'He's lost his marbles already; headship has got to him a bit more quickly than most!'*

No, I am perfectly sane. Few students look forward to the review, to the end of unit test or to the revision period. Many, often those who are relatively successful in such situations, recognise the value of such lessons, but excitement is not an emotion traditionally associated with tests. Some of the techniques described in this chapter can induce such emotions amongst students; more than one teacher has confirmed this and one teacher of A Level Further Maths claimed that high-flying students of his produced their best-ever work using an idea described in this chapter.

The techniques are set out under three major headings - *Reviewing, Testing* and *Revising* - but most readers will appreciate that it is often difficult to differentiate between reviewing and testing, or testing and revising. The examples, in practice, can apply in all three situations and the only function of the headings is to highlight the contexts in which good active whole-class teaching techniques can be used.

1 Reviewing

In my in-service work with schools over many years I made a habit of asking teachers how many of them began a lesson during an on-going topic with a few minutes of review - *'...what did we do last time?'* Most teachers, in all phases of education, agreed that they did.

Some adopt the *'I am going to remind you of what we did last time'* approach where the students go automatically into a passive frame of mind while the teacher talks and they look interested whilst thinking of something else (mental truancy).

Some choose the *'What did we do last time? Hands up'* approach and the volunteer/conscript game starts again. Most students do little thinking and even less speaking.

Some teachers are much more imaginative.

Ground Rule 8 in Chapter One described the use of the *Support Groups*, small groups of students who are regularly asked to meet for a short time in order to clarify tasks or language with each other. Such groups can also be used by teachers to review together the key learning points from the previous lesson. In May of 1996 I explained the purpose and mechanics of such groups to the staff of a school in Scotland and when I returned in October of the same year to work with departments, one of the teachers of History described his use of the technique.

The Support Group Review   Example 32

Students arrive in the room and if the topic is an on-going one the teacher simply says *'What did we learn last lesson about what life was like in the trenches?'* and presses the play button on the small cassette recorder on his desk. The theme tune from *Mission Impossible* at a moderate volume now fills the classroom and the students know that they have until the theme tune finishes to agree the key learning points from last lesson. They quickly turn to their text books, they look at their notes and very soon they are negotiating in groups over what to include in their summary list. Peer coaching, debate, some argument and frantically scribbled notes characterise the activity during the four minutes before the tune fades away. Everyone is now ready.

'Group One, give me one of your key points,' asks the teacher.

'Good, who else had that? Well done those groups.

Group Two, give me another of yours.'

This process continues, until all the key points are displayed on the blackboard. During this short session the teacher intervenes where necessary, seeking clarification or examples to check understanding, but the whole process lasts no more than ten minutes and he then proceeds with the teaching of new content or skills.

Music does not have to be used, of course, because the technique will work well without. If you do use music, however, be cautious over your choice of music - *Heavy Metal* may produce the wrong response!

My thanks to Mark Jones of Forres Academy, near Inverness for this example.

The Support Group Review technique has a number of learning benefits:

➡ It is a superb start to a lesson where there is little preamble, students know the procedure (ground rules in action!) and the music acts both as a starting pistol and as a stimulant.

➡ The students make use of notes and text book information but they have to make sense of it in order to produce a summary point.

➡ They remind each other, teach each other on occasions and by so doing consolidate their own learning.

➡ They enjoy it.

➡ It can be used with any age group and subject and can be used in conjunction with the Snowball Technique where the key ideas are arrived at in three stages, individual, pair and then Support Group.

➡ It can help inexperienced teachers to settle classes down quickly, creating the work ethic in the first few minutes of a lesson.

● ● ● ● ●

Support Group Review 2 - Them and You   Example 33

This example has many similarities to the *Support Group Review* described above. The main difference in this example is that the teacher also produces a set of key learning points. It works like this:

Stage 1 *'What did we learn last lesson about the properties of the chemicals x,y, z....?'*

Stage 2 Students (with or without music) form support groups (or go into the three stages of the Snowball Technique) and in the time agreed identify as many key points as they can. During this time the teacher is also recording key points onto an overhead transparency (OHT).

Stage 3 The teacher, using the overhead projector, reveals one of her key points. *'Which group has also chosen this?'* asks the teacher. The groups respond and the teacher interrogates them as necessary.

Stage 4 The remaining key points on the teacher's OHT are revealed and the process repeated.

Stage 5 The teacher's list is complete and the teacher invites groups to suggest key points that she did not choose.

Stage 6 A list of key points is agreed and, if felt necessary, students copy them down as a revision sheet. The lesson then proceeds.

This version of the Support Group Review has all the benefits of Example 32 but it also introduces an element of competition - students actually enjoy the challenge of seeing if they can match the teacher's choices and, if possible, think of points that the teacher fails to mention.

● ● ● ● ●

All teachers in their training will have been advised to try and create the right work atmosphere early in a lesson and in both the examples above students are quickly on task. Another strategy for teachers to achieve this is to begin the lesson in an unusual way. The following example illustrates such a technique.

Example 34   **Whole-Class Target-Setting**

Examples 32 and 33 are really effective ways of starting a lesson - students go straight into an activity creating the right atmosphere for productive teaching and learning. This example is also a super way to start a lesson. Whenever teachers hand back marked homework or assignments they listen to the ritual discussion where students eagerly enquire of each other:

'What did you get?'

The homework or assignment is then forgotten, unless it is a piece of coursework in which case teachers collect it back in and file it. All the comments, suggestions and hints about future practice is forgotten and the ten hours of marking that went into that set of scripts is almost entirely wasted.

In this example the comments and suggestions are the first things students have to think about as soon as work is returned to them.

At Blurton High School, the school where I am the Headteacher, all teachers will soon be making use of rubber stamps for their recording of assessments - an idea I first came across in the Science Department of Sir Graham Balfour School in Stafford, for which I am eternally grateful.

The rubber stamps contain three headings - *Content, Effort* and *Presentation,* each of which is given a grade or mark. This principle will apply to all staff, but the application of the principle will vary as individual departments adopt practice to suit subjects, levels and preferences. A fourth heading, *Target,* is at the bottom of the stamp, and under this heading all teachers will add a personal target for each student every time work is marked, a target that should enable students to improve on previous best, is attainable but not too demanding that it leads to demoralisation. Some students, of course, will be capable of more than one target and teachers will do their best to challenge students in this respect.

🛡️ **Blurton H.S.**	
CONTENT	3
EFFORT	4
PRESENTATION	3
TARGET	

As soon as the work is handed back all students as a whole-class activity are expected to look at the comments on the work, ask for guidance where something is not clear and then to move the target(s) physically from the bottom of that page to the top of the next.

XXXXXXXX XXX XXXXXXX XXXXXXXX
XXXXX XXXXXXXXXXX XXXXXX XX
XX XXXXXXXXXX XXXXXXXXXXXXXXX
XXXXXXXX XXXXXXXXXXXXX
XXXXXXXX XXXXXXXXX XXX XXX XXX
XXX XXXXXXXXXX XXXXXXX XXXX
XXXXXXXXXX XXXXX
XXXXXXX XXXXXXXXXXX XXXXXXXX XX
XXXX XXXXXXXXXXX XXXXXXXXXX

XXXXXX XXXXX XXX
XXXXXXXXXXX XXXXX
XXX X XXXXX XXX
X XXXXXXXXX
XXXXXXX XXXXXX
XXXX XXXX XXXX
XXXXXXXX XX XXX

XXX XXXXXXXXXXXXX
XXXXX XXXXXXXXX XXXX
XXXXXXX XXXXXX XXXXXXX XXXXXX
XX XXXXXX XXXXXX XXXXXX
XXXXXXX XXXXX XXXXXX XXXX XXX
XXXX XXX XXXXXX XXXXX XXXX XX
XXXX XXXXXXXXXXXX XXXXX XXXX
XXXXX XXXXX XX XXX XXXX XXXXX X
XXXXXX XXXXX
XXXXXX XXXXXXXXXX XXXXXX XXXX
XXXXXXXXXX XXXXXXX XXXXXX
XXXX XXXX XXXX XXXXXXXXXXXX
XXXXXXXXX XXXXXXXXX XXXX XXXX

Purpose

I must use more evidence

XXXXX X XX XXX XXX XX XX XXX
XXX XXX XX XX XXX XXXXX XXXX
XXXX XXXXX XXXX XXXX XXXX XXX
XX X X X XXX X XX X XX X
XXXXXX XXXXXXXXXX XXXX
XX XXX XXX XXX X X X
XX XXXX
X XX XXX XXX XXXX XXX XXX XXX
X XXX XX
XX X XX X X X X X
X X X X XXXXXX XXXXXX XXXXXX
XX XXXXXXX XXXXXX XXXXXX XXXX
XXXXXXX XXXXXXXXX XX X X XX
XXX XX X XXX XXX X XXXXXX XXXX
XXX XXXXX XX XX XX X X X
X X X XXXXX XX X XX XX X X X X
X X X XXXXXXXX XXXXX XXX X X
XXX X X X X X X X X X XX X X
X X X XXXXXX XX X X XXXXXX XXX
XXX XXX XXX XXXX XXXX X X X
XXXX X X XX X XXXXX XX X X X X
XX X XXXXX XX X XX.

🏵 Blurton H.S.	
CONTENT	3
EFFORT	4
PRESENTATION	3
TARGET	

Please try to use more evidence to support your conclusions

On Target

◎

Blurton
High School

Note that when the student achieves the target, a merit is awarded.

Rubber Stamps for Education are available from RBS Associates, Meadows House, Ampleforth Drive, Stafford ST17 4TE.
Tel: 01785 254859

So all students will start new pieces of work with one or more personal targets, useful for ensuring differentiation, and when the teacher next marks the work she will be reminded of the target and

On Target

Blurton High School

will look out for it during the assessment. If students, in the opinion of the teacher, have achieved their targets they are awarded a merit in the form of an attractively designed sticker which has the school logo printed on it. When students receive a set number of merits - decided by individual departments - they receive a departmental certificate of achievement, also attractively designed, which they can take home to show parents.

Each departmental certificate is reported to the Tutor and a record of this by subject is now placed on a large achievement poster for that class. (See illustration below.)

Blurton High School

Record of Subject Certificates

Year 7

7M1

Stacie Allert	*French*	*History*	*R.S.*		
Jodie Amos	*Science*	*I.C.T.*	*Music*		
Lee Birks	*Maths*	*Art*			
Adam Davis	*English*	*P.E.*	*Technology*	*Geography*	

My thanks to Blurton High School for allowing me to use these ideas.

Merit stickers and achievement posters like the ones shown, are available from The Merit Sticker Company of Barnet, Herts, who also produce achievement certificates and bookmarks in schools' own designs. For a brochure please telephone: 0181 441 2011.

When ten departmental certificates have been awarded from a combination of subjects, students receive a whole-school certificate in assembly and an achievement postcard is sent home.

Times Table Jigsaw   Example 35

Many teachers will have started lessons with an oral activity where students either as a whole class or individually recite their tables. In this example the teacher uses a novel approach.

Stage 1 Students are presented with a normal timestables grid like the one below.

1	2	3	4	5	6	7	8	9	10	11	12
2	4	6	8	10	12	14	16	18	20	22	24
3	6	9	12	15	18	21	24	27	30	33	36
4	8	12	16	20	24	28	32	36	40	44	48
5	10	15	20	25	30	35	40	45	50	55	60
6	12	18	24	30	36	42	48	54	60	66	72
7	14	21	28	35	42	49	56	63	70	77	84
8	16	24	32	40	48	56	64	72	80	88	96
9	18	27	36	45	54	63	72	81	90	99	108
10	20	30	40	50	60	70	80	90	100	110	120
11	22	33	44	55	66	77	88	99	110	121	132
12	24	36	48	60	72	84	96	108	120	132	144

Stage 2 They are then asked, maybe in pairs, to cut the square up into groups of four (or some other size) numbers so that they might end up with groupings such as:

30	40		40	45	50
33	44		48		

	14	21	28	35			10
						18	20
							30

Each pair of students should now have a set of 36 pieces of a jigsaw.

Stage 4 The 36 pieces are shuffled, placed in an envelope and handed to another pair of students.

Stage 5 Each pair has to re-form, as quickly as possible, the grid they have been given.

The difficulty level of the task can be amended in a number of ways:

- *Harder* by putting the timestables out of sequence before cutting.

- *Harder* by doing the 11 to 20 timestables.

- *Easier* by replacing the timestables grid with a simple number grid.

Teachers who do not want to have the bother of issuing and collecting scissors can prepare the jigsaw in advance, handing out envelopes with the grid already cut into pieces. (It is a good idea to code each jigsaw set with a letter so that sets do not become mixed up and the envelopes can be used again without re-organising.)

My thanks to Mick Tait, Head of Maths at Hagley Park High School in Rugeley for sending in this example. It is one of a number of activities that he used which are based on ideas found in the excellent 'Maths and School Magazine' published by the Mathematical Association.

● ● ● ● ●

Post-it Note   Example 36

This novel approach to reviewing learning is guaranteed to capture the attention of the students.   The activity is here being used in History but would work equally well in any subject with any age group.

Stage 1 The teacher asks a volunteer to come out to a chair at the front of the class. The teacher then places a Post-it note on the forehead of the volunteer and on it the teacher has written a key word or date. (In other subjects it could be a formula, a line from a poem, a chemical, a process, a product, equipment etc.) The word in this example is *Somme*.

Stage 2 The only person who cannot see what is written on the note is the volunteer who now has ten questions to find out what is written on the note. She is only allowed to ask questions that lead to a 'yes' or 'no' answer and so the questions must be framed in such a way that this is possible - 'Is this word a person? Is this word a treaty? Is this word a battle?'

Stage 3 As the volunteer fires questions at the class, the teacher (or another student), who is 'chairing' the proceedings, chooses who will respond to each question.

Stage 4 The volunteer may or may not discover the word within the ten questions limit but at the end someone else is called out, a new word, phrase or date is placed on her forehead and the process is repeated.

This review technique has a number of learning benefits:

➡ It develops thinking skills.

➡ It encourages students to use logic in order to solve the problem. Students have to listen carefully.

➡ It develops the ability to recall key knowledge quickly.

➡ It is a useful way of re-visiting key language or vocabulary.

➡ It is fun.

My thanks to Mark Jones, teacher of History at Forres Academy near Inverness, who first suggested this technique to me.

Example 37   **Building Language in Shakespeare**

In this example the teacher has been studying Romeo and Juliet with the class and begins the lesson by reviewing previous learning.

Stage 1 She places an OHT on the screen and brainstorms with the class, possibly using the Snowball Technique, the reasons for Tybalt's anger:

Tybalt

Why is he angry?

Who is Tybalt angry with?

Why is Capulet having a party?

Who is invited to the party?

Who isn't invited?

Why aren't Romeo and Mercutio discovered gatecrashing straightaway?

What happens at the party?

What happens next?

Tybalt is angry at Capulet's party

Stage 2 The class is asked to look again at the OHT and pick one word that best sums up the illustration - eg 'Anger'.

Stage 3 In small groups they are given a few minutes to develop a spider diagram around the key word anger, using words that are relevant to the play.

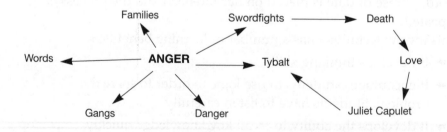

Stage 4 The class then plays one or more of the word games below using their knowledge of the play to assist them.
For example:

Word trains - where each word must have a logical link to the previous one in the 'train'.
Anger - violence

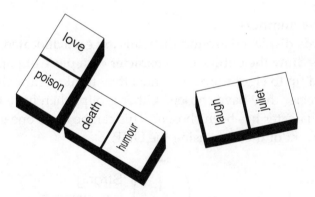

Word dominoes - where the connecting words must have a link with each other.

Word boxes
Students are asked to fill a box with lots of describing words

<blockquote>
fearful

angry

              strong

hateful   loving

quarrelsome   jealous

forgetful   just

etc...
</blockquote>

Alternatively, this box is compiled by the teacher with contributions from the class onto an OHT or a blackboard. These words can then be displayed around the classroom on pieces of paper or card.

The class then plays another game in **pairs:**

Stage 1 Player One thinks of a character and chooses 4 or 5 words from the word box to describe that character.

Stage 2 Player Two has to guess the character in as few guesses as possible.

The game can be played in **groups.** It is the same game as the one above except each group chooses a range of characters, selects the words and then exchanges its words with other groups who have to guess the characters.

Words by numbers
The words displayed around the walls are each allocated a number. Students draw the outline of a character on a piece of paper and then add up to eight numbers which they think accurately describe the character they have chosen. Other groups then have to guess which character has been chosen. This can be done one group at a time in front of the class using the OHP.

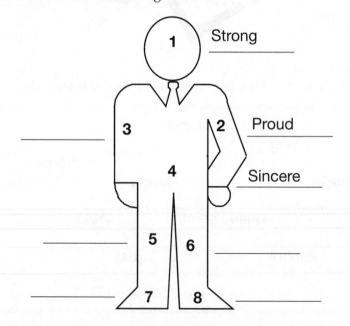

Words must fit the character, however, and other groups or the teacher can challenge any group to justify its choices. For example, one group uses the words *'strong'* and *'weak'* and is asked to explain why this character is both of these things.

This review exercise fulfils a number of functions:

➡ It helps students to recall characters and events from the play.

➡ It encourages participation.

➡ It is a good example of how a sequence of activities can be devised where each stage builds upon the last and where the degree of challenge increases stage by stage.

➡ It provides opportunities for group discussion, negotiation and debate and in so doing students coach each other.

➡ It is a superb example of how teachers can use time twice - the activity reinforces knowledge and understanding of the play and also contributes centrally to the building of language and vocabulary.

My thanks to Andrew McPherson for this example. Andrew has published a range of superb resources which promote and develop language. Further details are available from: Cutting Edge Publications, Pill Farmhouse, Lostwithiel, Cornwall PL22 0JR. Tel: 01208 872337.

2 Testing

Teachers use tests for a variety of purposes:
(a) To assess understanding or skills.
(b) To evaluate the effectiveness of a teaching programme.
(c) To compare the relative progress of students.
(d) To place students or a school against locally or nationally defined norms.
(e) To give practice to students preparing for external examinations or tests.
The examples that follow in this section deal with (a) and (b) above - where teachers are using a test to assess the understanding of students and/or to discover whether the teaching approach used has been effective. There are, however, a number of problems with testing that need to be addressed before we look at the various techniques that can be adopted.

Some tests do not assess understanding but rather the ability of students to find the right answer.
I dealt with this issue in Chapter Three of Book One in the series, *Raising Achievement.* I pointed out that some tests, usually written ones, are dominated by the asking of questions, or by exercises that involve students in low-level tasks like the filling in of missing words. Students become fairly adept at such tasks, but this 'success' is often exposed by an external examination which sets out to test deeper understanding.

Some students have a good understanding of the topic but do badly in the test because the language used is inaccessible.
The example used in Book One is worth repeating here:

> *'Name an instrument that is used to measure temperature.'*
> *'Trombone.'*

The student here has a reading age of six but recognises the word *instrument* because her music teacher has taught the class the key vocabulary. The Science teacher has not and therefore some students will do badly in this test not because they are poor at Science but because they have limited vocabulary. When students are faced with situations like this their self-esteem takes a battering and it is no wonder that some come to have a genuine fear and loathing of tests.

Some students are unable to translate the thoughts they have in their heads into words onto a page.
It must be incredibly frustrating, and ultimately demoralising, for students to enjoy a lesson, understand the topic, participate in the discussion and then be unable to record that understanding because the medium required, *writing*, is their main weakness. Written tests in some classes will invoke these soul-destroying emotions in students, and, as the Elton Report on behaviour and discipline pointed out, some will eventually opt out of a system that constantly defeats them.

The examples that follow will not eradicate such problems - only a long-term programme of language development will do that - but they will provide opportunities for both teachers and students to experience testing that is enjoyable, where understanding can be conveyed in a variety of ways, where participation is high and where the process of assessment enables students to consolidate their learning.

Many teachers seem unaware that the process of formulating a question is itself a learning activity; that to ask a good question demonstrates an understanding of the subject. Most of the questions asked in classrooms are posed by the teacher for students, and so if asking questions involves learning, it is not unreasonable to conclude that many teachers, by asking questions, are re-inforcing what they already know. It does not always have to be like that.

Hot Seating   Example 38

Hot Seating is used widely by teachers of English and Drama and can be used by teachers of all subjects and all age groups.   Traditionally, at the end of a section or a topic teachers will test understanding by throwing questions at the class. In Hot Seating the questions are posed by students for other students.

Stage 1 The teacher explains that there is now going to be a test on the learning that has taken place. She chooses a small group of students to be in the 'hot seat'. (Some teachers will ask one student alone to be in the hot seat. That is fine if the class is one that has confident and articulate students, but in some classes individuals would be terrified to be placed on the spot on their own, and will participate more willingly in the security of the group.)

Stage 2 The rest of the class are formed into groups and told that they must prepare questions on the topic for the 'experts' in the hot seat. The teacher insists that no questions will be allowed unless those asking have also prepared the answers.

Stage 3 The hot seat group revises the topic, trying to anticipate questions and the remaining groups try to think of appropriate and challenging questions.

Stage 4 When groups have come up with good questions and what they think are 'correct' answers they ask the teacher to scrutinise them and pass them as suitable. If not, the group has to re-think or amend the questions until the teacher is happy. The hot seat group continues to talk, revising and thinking up answers to imaginary questions.

Stage 5 The teacher chairs the test with each group in turn putting its questions to the hot seat group while the teacher adjudicates proceedings.

Stage 6 The teacher can change the hot seat group at any time with comments such as '...*that was a good question from that group, so good, in fact, that I think they should now be in the hot seat*'.

This approach to testing has enormous learning benefits:

➡ Learning is now widespread as those questioning and those responding all remenber the key points.

➡ Students have a natural desire to ask questions of their friends that they can't answer, so the process actually encourages students to go to the limit of their own understanding.

➡ Peer coaching is taking place both in the hot seat group (revising together) and in the groups posing questions ('*Let's ask... Why? Because it...*')

➡ Once again it's a learning activity that is enjoyed by all.

Example 39   **True or False?**

Working in groups or pairs students are asked to prepare for a test by studying the topic in detail and then producing a series of statements. For example, in A Level Sociology the statements might include:

> '*There is no evidence that educational achievement is linked to social class.*'
> '*The Education Act of 1944 introduced comprehensive education.*'
> '*The data on gender and educational achievement suggests that boys consistently out-perform girls in Mathematics and Science but that in the Arts girls achieve more highly.*'
> '*The 1988 Education Reform Act in England and Wales was introduced by the then Secretary of State for Education, John Patten.*'

As each statement is produced it is copied onto a sheet and distributed to the other groups who have to decide whether it is true or false. Each group must prepare evidence to support its conclusion.

Eventually the teacher leads a plenary where each statement is read out and other groups attack or defend it as being true or false. Many, of course, will be partially true and the teacher will try to draw out these subtle points.

Spot the Concept   Example 4C

In this example students are asked to study the topic in preparation for a test on conceptual language or terminology.

Stage 1 Students revise on their own.

Stage 2 When the revision period is over they work in pairs to produce a series of definitions, examples or situations which relate to a key concept or technical term.

Stage 3 When everyone is ready each pair reads out one of their definitions and the other students must record what they think is the key concept or technical term.

Stage 4 The teacher now leads the marking of the test, inviting each pair to offer an answer and then asking others whether they agree.

Stage 5 Corrections are made where necessary and an accurate revision sheet is produced.

My thanks to David Abbott from Burwell, Cambridgeshire, a teacher of 'A' Level Sociology, for Examples 39 and 40.

Example 41   **Sabotage**

This example is very similar to the ones above. Small groups of students study the topic and then prepare a written or oral presentation on one aspect. They build into the presentation one or more deliberate errors of fact, process or logic. The other groups have to spot the error(s), explain the mistake(s) to the class and produce an accurate version. The students will not always agree and the teacher acts as a broker, adjudicating where necessary. These last two activities have a number of learning benefits:

➡ The statements or presentations are arrived at after what should be intense scrutiny of the topic or data.

➡ Students will be keen to outwit their peers, and so quite subtle statements or errors will appear which will challenge everyone in deciding whether they are true or false, correct or erroneous. (It is not unknown for examiners to use the same tactic - subtle questions to catch out students who have been prepared with 'coached' responses.)

➡ They generally involve enjoyment and participation.

• • • • •

The example that follows is the longest in the book but it is on the subject of spelling and whole-class or whole-school policy, and with my views on the importance of language development well known I feel it is worth including in full.

A Whole-Class Spelling Policy

Example 42

Stage 1 Make sure that your policy on marking and on correcting work is understood not only by students but by parents. The example below is stuck on the inside cover of the exercise book.

How I Am Going To Help You With Your Writing

When you write, the most important thing is to explain everything well, so that someone reading your work can understand what you mean. I will write comments under your work, or at the side, to help you with this.

It is also important to write in proper sentences, with full stops and capital letters. This helps to make your meaning clear. If you miss out a full stop, I will put one in the margin of the line where you missed it out. You must look at that line of writing, see where it needs to go, and put it in. Of course, you will need a capital letter after it.

Spelling is important too. If you can't spell a word I think you should know, I will write `sp ' (for spelling) in the margin, and underline the word. I will write the word on the last page of your book. You must correct your mistake and learn the word. If you get it wrong again, you will have to write it out five times.

For hard words which I don't expect you to know, I will write the word in your margin. Correct it, and learn it if you can, but I don't mind if you can't.

If you have a lot of difficulty with writing, I won't correct every mistake. I will correct what I want you to learn first, and when you know these words, I will start correcting more. ALWAYS DO YOUR CORRECTIONS! I WILL CHECK!

Stage 2 Make the first page of the exercise book a contents page and leave a column marked *'corrections'*. (You'll see why later.)

Contents

Date	Title	Corrections
19/9/95	Opaque and Transparent Materials	G Kennedy
26/9/95	Experiment to Show Light Travels in Straight Lines	G Kennedy
19/9/95	Light Sources	G Kennedy
3/10/95	Experiment to Use a Mirror to Bend a Ray of Light	G Kennedy
3/10/95	Shadows	G Kennedy
10/10/95	Shadow Challenge	G Kennedy
17/10/95	Moon	G Kennedy
17/10/95	How We See Light	G Kennedy
17/10/95	How We See Light reflected in a Mirror	G Kennedy
31/10/95	Continents	G Kennedy
7/11/95	Some Countries In Each Continent	G Kennedy
14/11/95	Latitude	G Kennedy
21/11/95	Our Countries	G Kennedy
28/11/95	Co-ordinates	G Kennedy
9/1/96	What I Already Know About the Sun, Moon and Earth	G Kennedy
9/1/96	What I Learned from the Programme	G Kennedy
16/1/96	The Moon	G Kennedy
23/1/96	Our Solar System	G Kennedy
6/2/96	Classifying Materials	G Kennedy
13/2/96	Natural and Man-Made Materials	G Kennedy
27/2/96	Properties of Materials	G Kennedy
5/3/96	Materials and their Uses	G Kennedy

Stage 3 Make the final page of the exercise book a spellings page. Call it *'words I must learn to spell'*.

Stage 4 When marking work choose a number of mis-spelled words for students to learn. Be realistic - two or three is probably enough. These words become the 'target' for the student.

Stage 5 Underline each mis-spelling and write *Sp* in the margin.
Write these words correctly on the back page.

Example:

sp

Experiment to Find Temperature of water in   Tuesday 19ᵗʰ March
a Class Insulated with foil
In the experiment we filled a Class with water and covered it with
foil and put a thermometer in it. And every minuite we just
wrote down the temperature

Comparing Thermal Insulators

Insulator	Water Temperature After	
	5 mins	10 mins
Paper	4.7 °C	45 °C
Nothing	44 °C	42 °C
Cotten	48 °C	-
Foil	45 °C	42 °C
wool	46½ °C	45 °C

SP

The table of results show that after 5 minuets the best
thermal insulator was cotten and the worst was nothing. After
10 minuetes, the best insulators were wool and paper the worst
insulators were nothing and cotten.

SP
sp
SP

Stage 6 When the exercise books are returned, students look up the correct spellings on the back page, they then cross out the mis-spellings and write in the correct spellings above. Note how the students have to remember the spellings for a few seconds while turning back.

Example:

```
Experiment to Find Temperature of water in   Tuesday 19th March
a Glass Insulated with foil
In the experiment we filled a Glass with water and covered it with
sp  foil and put a thermometer in it. And every minute we just
    wrote down the temperature          minute


Comparing Thermal Insulators
  Insulator          Water Temperature After
                     5 mins        10 mins
     Paper            47°C          45°C
     Nothing          44°C          42°C
sp   Cotter Cotten    48°C           -
     Foil             45°C          42°C
     wool             46½°C         45°C
     The table of results show that after 5 minuets the best
sp   thermal insulator was cotton and the worst was nothing. After
sp   10 minutes, the best insulators were wool and paper the worst
sp   insulators were nothing and cotton
```

Stage 7 Give the whole class a few minutes to learn the spellings individually or in pairs.

Stage 8 When you next mark the books sign the Contents Page if all corrections from the last piece of work have been done, (see illustration at stage 2) thus the importance of the 'corrections' column.

Stage 9 When you mark the books again look up the list of spellings. Any words mis-spelt again must be written out five times by the student on the back page. You just write 5x against the word. Students do try to avoid extra work by being *careful* not to make the same mistake twice.

Stage 10 Do re-visit the word list regularly, at the beginning, in the middle of a double period, or at the end of lessons so that students come to acquire the vocabulary through *constant* usage.

This policy has a number of learning benefits:

- It soon becomes a routine for the students that is performed quickly and carefully.
- Spelling tests can now take place with pairs of students testing each other on words that are appropriate to individuals.
- Students can see for themselves how their vocabulary is growing.
- Parents will understand the system and can involve themselves if they wish.
- Other staff, like the Form Tutor or guidance teacher, can celebrate the achievements of the students.
- It provides teachers with a starting routine that settles the class down immediately their books are returned.
- It can operate in a mixed ability or setted situation because each list is individualised.
- It integrates well with a policy of key language being displayed on walls and worksheets.
- It can be operated in all subjects and at all levels of ability.

My thanks for this example to Gill Minikin, Learning Support Teacher, at Chalfonts Community College, Bucks.

● ● ● ● ●

In the previous example students were required at one stage to test each other, and there is no doubt that in the process of testing others the testers are also consolidating their own learning. In the next example this idea is extended to include the assessment of oral work.

Oral work is notoriously difficult to assess, particularly in a large class where there are some students, the *'volunteers'* who speak often and with confidence, and others, the *'conscripts'* whose contributions are few and often limited to 'I'm not sure...' or other short utterances. The example below illustrates the ingenious ways that teachers find both to encourage participation in oral work and to involve students in its assessment.

Example 43	Assessment of Oral Work

In this example from English, the teacher has organised an extended role play of a school governors' meeting which relates to events in a play called *The Thief* by Jan Needle. Fifteen students prepare their given roles using details from the play to gather information. Meanwhile, the other half of the class devise their own assessment sheets in order that they can assess one student each in terms of how well they fulfilled their part. The teacher takes on the role of Headteacher in the final role play.

During the role play, all students are occupied because the role playing students are sat around a circle of desks in the centre of the classroom, and assessing students are sitting around the outside of the classroom.

In the next lesson the assessing students each give a small presentation on the particular student they were observing. While they do this, the teacher can be assessing them on the strength, delivery and accuracy of their observations. The students' assessments of the role players, if accurate and fair, can be used by the teacher in an overall assessment.

This activity has a number of points to commend it:

➡ Participation of all students in oral work has been achieved.

➡ Speaking and listening skills have been developed and assessed.

➡ Students have to understand and use the assessment criteria and this will help them in preparation for external examinations.

➡ Time is being used twice; understanding of the play, research skills, assessment skills and oral and listening skills, all in one activity!

➡ Students, according to the author of the example, enjoy the experience.

My thanks for this example to Craig J Ennew, teacher of English at Bishop Wordsworth's School in Salisbury.

3 Revising

Activities designed for revision need to develop a number of skills in students:

- **Memory** - most external tests and examinations still test the ability to recall key data or information.
- **Speed of thought** - most tests and examinations demand (unfortunately) that students work to tight time deadlines.
- **Interpretation** - memory will count for little if students are unable to interpret questions, to make sense of data or to apply facts, formulae or skills in new contexts.
- **Deeper understanding** - coached responses will only ever achieve low grades whereas students who really understand topics will score more highly as they demonstrate higher order skills and responses.

The examples that follow illustrate some of the approaches that can be used to develop one or more of these skills.

Test the Other Half	Example 44

In this example from Modern Languages the teacher is testing oral skills along with simple structures and vocabulary. Periodically the class is given a test on the language recently covered but the test is not set by the teacher but by one half of the class for the other. There are a number of ways in which this can be organised but the approach described works well.

The class is divided into two 'equal' teams, Left and Right, where each team has been selected carefully by the teacher to reflect the range of skills and confidence in the class. Each week the teams have to prepare a test for the other half of the class. For homework all students have to prepare their question(s) and they can be presented in a number of ways:

(1) An illustration or photograph (eg of a fruit) where students have to use the french word - ' *une pomme'*.
(2) A word or phrase in the target language where students have to identify the correct product or situation from a range of photographs or collages displayed on the wall. So, for example, the Left team might have to respond to an oral question from the Right team *'Avez-vous une chambre pour deux personnes avec bain?'* by writing down the response displayed on the wall *'Oui, nous avons une chambre pour deux personnes avec bain'*.
(3) A mimed action where students have to decide what is being mimed and select the correct phrase from a number listed on the wall eg *'tu as mal à la tête'*.

The test is marked immediately and scores for each person are aggregated and recorded on a chart or graph on the wall (see illustration).The teacher can modify the process easily, choosing the context for the test, insisting on particular structures eg *'Je n'aime pas les pommes'* etc.

This type of test has a number of learning benefits for both the tester and the tested.

Students revise with a real purpose in mind.They learn from asking as well as answering. They have to think quickly. They want to beat the other side so ask challenging questions, but revise carefully so that they aren't themselves caught out. They have to apply recently acquired language. They practise different language skills eg speaking, intonation, listening, copywriting, memorisation, comprehension, writing.

Pictogramme   Example 45

This example is also taken from Modern Languages but involves a more open-ended approach to testing than Example 44 which involved fairly closed questioning. In this activity students are asked to prepare for homework a storyboard on a topic that has recently been studied by the class, eg *L'office de tourisme'*. Each storyboard must have two parts, eg tourist and receptionist, and students must prepare a story that involves dialogue between the two.

Stage 1 All students prepare storyboards on the chosen topic.

Stage 2 The lesson starts with the teacher dividing the class into pairs.

Stage 3 The first student shows her storyboard to her partner. She will have prepared the language for both parts in the story but takes only one part, eg the tourist, and her partner has to reply to what is said, using the illustrations in the storyboard to guide him. The first student assesses the language of her partner.

Example of conversation : À l'office de tourisme

Stage 4 The second student then shows his storyboard to the first student and the process is reversed.

This class activity can be organised so that all students do this at the same time in their own pairs or it can become a class activity where pairs conduct their conversations at the front of the class, possibly displaying their storyboards on an OHP. If this approach is adopted other students can participate if individuals have any difficulty, and there are also opportunities for students to suggest different or more complex interpretations of the storyboard.

This example has the same learning benefits as Example 43 but in addition:

- Its greater open-endedness offers students wider opportunities to demonstrate their skills in using language.
- It allows a limited amount of role play.
- It demands that students not only learn vocabulary and structures but also practise using them in real contexts.
- The students practise different language skills as well as the defined language.
- They carry out peer assessment and if the criteria for success is discussed in class they learn to identify the kinds of responses needed for particular grades or marks.

Revision Exercises

Many students understand the importance of revision but find it boring, with many unable to organise themselves sufficiently to make it a productive process. Many schools will send students home for study leave during the weeks before the external examinations begin and while some students use this time well many will find it difficult to go beyond the reading and re-reading of notes or examples. When this happens anxiety can increase and with it a feeling of fatalism - *'revision is a waste of time and it's now all down to luck on the day'*. The examples that follow in this section examine a range of strategies for making revision both effective and fun. Although they are presented in this book as whole-class teaching activities, many of the techniques can be used by students at home or in revision sessions with friends.

Trigger words

All of the examples that follow make use of a technique that is successfully used by many teachers and students. The technique is to divide the content that has to be revised into a number of sections and then to sub-divide each of these sections in the same way. All sections and sub-sections should then be allocated *trigger words* (or formulae or symbols) which will be used by students to remind them of the content.

For example, in a unit on Healthy Eating the trigger words for main sections might include *Protein, Sugars, Fat* and *Heart Disease*. The sub-headings for Protein might include *growth, repair, animal, plant*, etc.

Once students have decided upon their trigger words the task of revision is made more orderly with the memorising of words rather than pages of text a less daunting task. That is not the end of the process, however. Being able to memorise words is of no use unless students can go beyond them into meaning and interpretation, and that is where the activities that follow become useful.

Mastery   Example 46

In this example a test is devised by the teacher on a chosen topic.

Stage 1 The teacher prepares a test in four parts to cover the four sections of the topic. The key 'trigger' words for each section are displayed on the wall.

Stage 2 The teacher divides the class into groups of four with each group chosen carefully to reflect the full range of ability and confidence found in the class.

Stage 3 The teacher explains that groups must revise for the test together and can only be awarded their 'mastery certificates' once all members of the group have achieved the set standard (eg 80%).

Stage 4 The students have a set period of time to revise in their groups, and during this period they must go beyond the words into examples, applications and meaning.

Stage 5 The first part of the test is completed and assessed. Mastery certificates are awarded to those who achieve the set standard.

Stage 6 The remaining parts of the test are conducted in the same way.

Stage 7 The teacher is able to organise tutorials or further revision sessions for those who have not achieved mastery certificates for each section.

The learning benefits are obvious:

- The key words act as triggers to the deeper meaning.
- Students are quite keen to be awarded the mastery certificates and therefore spend time in coaching and supporting members of the group who are finding some topics difficult.
- Students who have to explain concepts or facts or demonstrate skills to others consolidate their own learning in the process.
- Final revision sessions organised by the teacher can focus on the needs of individuals which is a better use of time than going through a topic with all students, many of whom don't need it.

Example 47   **The Challenge Game**

In this revision game teachers also make use of the trigger word technique.

Stage 1 Display the trigger words around the walls or on a flip chart.

Stage 2 The class is organised into small groups of three or four, given a number (eg group 1, group 2 etc) and told to revise in the same way as in Example 46.

Stage 3 Each group, once it has completed its revision, chooses three trigger words and prepares five questions for each of them.

Stage 4 The teacher issues three small rectangular pieces of overhead transparency cut to about 6 x 4 centimetres. Using a non-permanent overhead pen, the students write one of their chosen words on each of the three transparency pieces (see illustration).

| fibre | cholesterol | vitamins |

Stage 5 The teacher places a master transparency onto the screen with the topic placed in the centre. Around it are empty rectangular blocks (see illustration below).

Stage 6 Group 1 is invited by the teacher to display one of its chosen trigger words onto the overhead, filling one of the blank rectangles. Group 2 is invited to challenge Group 1 on that word; if Group 2 thinks it knows more about this word than Group 1 it accepts the challenge and asks its five questions. If Group 2 declines the challenge Group 3 is invited to challenge and so on... In all cases of a challenge the teacher intervenes if the question is deemed to be unfair.

Stage 7 Group 1 responds to whichever group is presenting the challenge and if it answers the five questions to the satisfaction of the teacher it wins one point for its team and the teacher records this on a scoreboard somewhere in the room. If Group 1 cannot answer any of the questions but the challenging group can, then the challenging group wins the point.

Stage 8 Each group in turn is then given the chance to display one of its words on the OHP screen and the same process is repeated until all the blank spaces are filled or until all the chosen trigger words are used up.

Stage 9 The group with the most points on the board once all the blank rectangles are filled wins the revision game.

This revision activity has a number of learning benefits:

- Students revise with a purpose.
- There is peer coaching and peer support in the preparation of the questions.
- Students learn both from *asking* and *answering* questions.
- Students go beyond the key words into deeper meaning and understanding.
- The desire to catch out the other groups means that students are sometimes going into quite complex and difficult aspects of the topic. This process can often result in a degree of challenge that some teacher tests would not have provided.

| Example 48 | Round the Class |

Stage 1 Trigger words are placed around the room by the teacher and students revise them thoroughly, trying as in the previous examples, to go beyond the word into meaning, application, significance etc.

Stage 2 The teacher asks the students to form a circle.

Stage 3 The teacher asks one student at random a question based on the trigger words. The student responds and if the teacher is happy with the answer the student scores a point.

Stage 4 This student now says something along the lines of '*I knew quite a lot about...*'(the question asked by the teacher)' *but what I'm confused about is...* and proceeds to ask another question. The next person in the circle has to respond. This student responds and the teacher asks the questioner if she is happy with the answer. The questioner says '*yes*' or '*no*'. If the questioner says '*yes*' but the teacher thinks that the answer was, in fact, an unsatisfactory one, then the questioner has a point deducted. If, on the other hand, the answer is '*no*', she has to give a better reply to her own question. If the teacher is happy with her reply then she is awarded another point, if not she has a point deducted.

Stage 5 The next student in the circle now repeats the process with '*The thing I would like to know is...*' and so on.

Stage 6 (Optional) The teacher has also prepared questions on all the trigger words and if students are successful in answering their questions they can opt for two bonus points by answering one of the teacher's questions. If they opt for the question but are unsuccessful they lose two points.

This activity is useful for revision because:
- It encourages students to study topics in depth.
- It provides opportunities for students to learn both by asking and by answering questions.
- Students enjoy catching out their peers and so students 'go for the jugular' in devising questions for others.
- All students are involved.
- The teacher is able to identify from the quality of both the questions and the answers which topics are well understood and which need further revision.

● ● ● ● ●

Example 49   Dominoes

Stage 1 The teacher prepares a range of trigger words and places them randomly onto cards, one on each end as in a game of dominoes (see illustration). A number of sets are prepared, all on different colour card so that they can be reorganised at the end of the lesson.

ALUMINIUM	MELTING POINT	BROMINE	BALLOONS	CALCIUM	PARTICLES
COPPER	RATE	CHLORINE	FOOD	HELIUM	CATALYST
IRON	RADIATION	LEAD	BOILING POINT	MAGNESIUM	METAL
MERCURY	NON–METAL	NITROGEN	LIQUID	OXYGEN	FERTILISER
PHOSPHORUS	PRESERVATIVE	POTASSIUM	ELECTRON	SODIUM	GAS
SULPHUR	ALKALI	TIN	REACTIVITY	ZINC	SALT

Stage 2 The cards in each set are shuffled and dealt out to groups of four or five students, with each student in the group having an equal number of cards.

Stage 3 One of the students starts the game by placing one of his cards down on the table, as in a game of dominoes. The next student in a clockwise direction is given the opportunity of placing one of her cards down if she is able to justify a link between the two words now juxtaposed (see illustration).

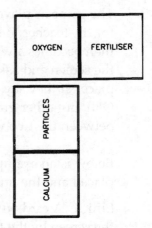

Stage 4 Other students in the group can challenge any student who thus places a card with the words 'explain the link'. If the student is able to explain the link then the card remains on the table; if not she has to take it back and the next student has his turn. In any dispute the teacher is called in to be adjudicator.

Stage 5 The game continues in the same way with students adding to the dominoes when their turn comes. The winner is the student who can place all his or her cards first, taking all challenges with confidence.

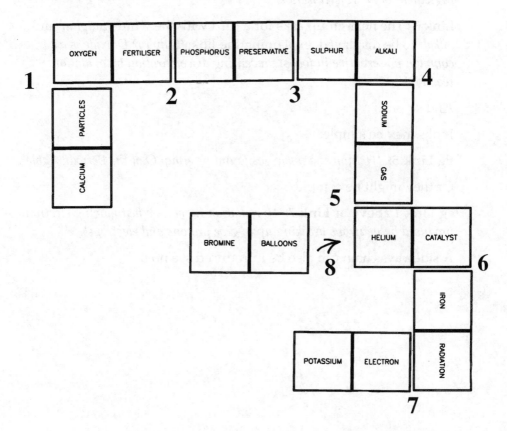

The game as played here is one for small groups but an alternative is for the teacher to have one set of the cards on transparencies and it then becomes a whole-class game. The teacher displays one card on the screen and asks Group 1 if they have a card they would like to place. If they say *'yes'* the teacher places their chosen card on the OHP but other groups can challenge if they cannot see a link between the two words juxtaposed.

Below is an example of what might take place with both the cards placed and the links established:

Link 1 A card with the words *Calcium* and *Particles* is displayed on the screen by the teacher. The next group asks him to display a card with the words *Oxygen* and *Fertiliser* next to them and explains the link thus: *'Oxygen is a gas because it has diatomic particles which are relatively stable, with little attraction for each other'*.

Link 2 The next group ask for a card with the words *Phosphorus* and *Preservative* to be displayed, explaining the link: *'Phosphorus is one ingredient of NPK fertilisers'*.

Link 3 The next group asks for a card with the words *Sulphur* and *Alkali* to be displayed, explaining the link: *'Sulphur Dioxide is a common preservative in foods, preventing discolouration by oxidation reactions'*.

And so on...

Links may be simple:

Eg Link 5: *'Helium is a noble gas found in group O of the Periodic Table'*.

Or they might be complex:

eg Link 1 above or Link 7: *'β radiation involves a fast moving electron produced by neutrons breaking up to give protons and electrons'*.

A sideways chain can also be introduced see no 8.

This revision game has a number of learning benefits:
- It is good for building key language and as such can be used early in a course for that purpose.
- It provides students with a visual stimulus which some will find useful in recalling key ideas.
- Students play the game in groups and learn from each other.
- The challenges enable students to articulate their understanding and both those challenging and those being challenged benefit.
- The game can be played by students with varying degrees of confidence because the links can be both simple and complex.

My thanks to Ursa Massam, formerly of Sir Graham Balfour School, Stafford, and now Head of Science at Edensor High School, Stoke-on-Trent, who took the dominoes idea and produced this example for me.

Prepare a Revision Pack   Example 50

I ran a whole-staff training session for a Sixth Form College in Yorkshire in December of 1996, and in February of 1997 was invited back to work with departments, many of whom were incorporating ideas introduced in December into existing schemes of work. The Head of Mathematics asked me to look at a piece of work produced by two students in his A Level Further Maths group. He had used the idea, presented frequently in this book, of asking students to test others. He had gone further, however, and had asked students to prepare a complete revision pack for other students, which had to include (a) a summary of the topic, (b) a test, (c) an answer sheet and mark scheme and (d) a detailed set of summary sheets for the test. The complete packs, one for each of three papers, are too long to reproduce here, but a sample from one unit is included which will give readers a flavour of what the students produced.

See illustration over page.

1 A sample of the first page

DIFFERENTIATION REVISION PACK (PAPER 1)

Topic Summary

Rate Of Change
- When a quantity is increasing, its rate of change is positive, and negative when it is decreasing.
- Rate of change is usually w.r.t. time, but it does not have to be. For example, the volume of a cylinder changes w.r.t. its length.

Local Linear Approximation & Gradient
- A very small section of a curve can be approximated to a line.

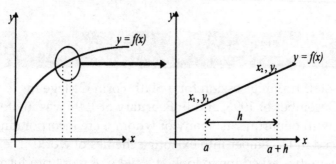

- The gradient of this line is given by the change in the y-value over the change in the x-value. On the curve $y = f(x)$, the gradient of the line between the points $x = a$ and $x = a + h$ is given by

$$\text{Gradient} \approx \frac{y_2 - y_1}{x_2 - x_1} \approx \frac{f(x_2) - f(x_1)}{x_2 - x_1} \approx \frac{f(a+h) - f(a)}{(a+h) - a} \approx \frac{f(a+h) - f(a)}{h}$$

- As h gets smaller, the approximation becomes more accurate. As h approaches zero, the value we calculate for the gradient approaches a limit. This is the exact gradient, and we have found the exact value of the rate of change of y w.r.t. x, also written as $f'(x)$, or $\frac{dy}{dx}$.

---

2   Questions 1, 4 and 5 of the test

Test On Differentiation

Q1. Find the following:

a) $\dfrac{d}{dx}(x^2 - 3x + 10)$

b) $\dfrac{d}{dx}(5x^2 e^{3x})$

c) $\dfrac{d}{dx}(e^c)$ where c is a constant

d) $\dfrac{d}{dw}(p \ln w)$ where p is a constant

e) $\dfrac{dy}{dx}$, given that $y = \dfrac{3e^{2x} + e^x}{4e^{2x} + e^{4x}}$

f) $\dfrac{dy}{dx}$, given that $y = 4u^2 + 3u - 7$ and $u = 6x + 2e^x$

Q4. A gibbon (a primate renowned for its unrealistically long arms) swings from a fixed point on a tall branch of his tree. At a time t seconds after he begins to swing, the horizontal distance x of the gibbon from the tree is given by $x = 7t^2 - t^3 + 8t + k$. He lands again after 8 seconds. Given that the gibbon starts from the base of his tree, find:

a) The value of k

b) The speed with which he jumps from the ground

c) The maximum horizontal speed he attains

d) The length of his arms, given that at the greatest distance reached, his arms are horizontal.

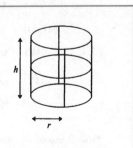

Q5. A prize-winning sculptor specialises in surreal miniatures. She wishes to create a model of a dead baked bean can, using 50cm of wire. The skeleton is to be made of 3 rings and 4 rods, as shown in the diagram. Obtain an expression for the volume of the can in terms of its radius and, given that the density of baked beans is 0.275 g cm^{-3}, find the greatest mass of baked beans an equivalent "live" can could hold, giving your answer to the nearest gram.

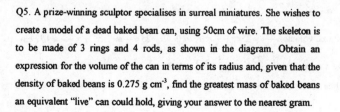

3 The answers and mark scheme for questions 1, 4 and 5.

Solutions And Mark Scheme

Q1

1...................(B1)   a) $2x - 3$

2.............(M1, A1)   b) $5xe^{3x}(2+3x)$

1...................(B1)   c) 0

1...................(B1)   d) $\dfrac{p}{w}$

3.............(M1, A2)   e) $-\dfrac{6e^{3x}+3e^{2x}+4}{e^{5x}+8e^{3x}+16e^{x}}$

2.............(M1, A1)   f) $18 + 288x + 102e^{x} + 96xe^{x} + 32e^{2x}$

Q4

1...................(B1)   a) $k = 0$

2.............(M1, A1)   b) $v = \dfrac{dx}{dt} = 14t - 3t^2 + 8 \quad \therefore \quad t = 0 \Rightarrow v = 8\,\mathrm{ms^{-1}}$

3.............(M2, A1)   c) $\dfrac{dv}{dt} = 14 - 6t \quad \therefore \quad$ maximum speed when $14 - 6t = 0 \therefore t = \dfrac{14}{6} = \dfrac{7}{3}\,\mathrm{s}$

$v = 14t - 3t^2 + 8 = 14 \times \dfrac{7}{3} - 3 \times \dfrac{49}{9} + 8 = \dfrac{73}{3} = 24.33\,\mathrm{ms^{-1}}$

3.............(M2, A1)   d) $\dfrac{dx}{dt} = 14t - 3t^2 + 8 \quad \therefore \quad$ maxiumum distance when $14t - 3t^2 + 8 = 0$

$t = \dfrac{-14 \pm \sqrt{196 + 96}}{-6} = 5.18\,\mathrm{s} \quad \therefore \quad x = 7t^2 - t^3 + 8t = 90.3\,\mathrm{m}$

Q5

1...................(M1)   Length of wire: $3 \times 2\pi r + 4h = 50$ Volume: $V = \pi r^2 h$

2.............(M1, A1) $\therefore \quad h = \dfrac{25 - 3\pi r}{2} \quad \therefore \quad V = \dfrac{25}{2}\pi r^2 - \dfrac{3}{2}\pi^2 r^3$

2...................(M2)   Maximum volume: $\dfrac{dV}{dr} = 25\pi r - \dfrac{9}{2}\pi^2 r^2 = 0 \quad \therefore \quad 25 = \dfrac{9}{2}\pi r \quad \therefore \quad r = \dfrac{50}{9\pi} \approx 1.77\,\mathrm{cm}$

1...................(M1)   giving a volume of $V = \dfrac{25}{2}\pi r^2 - \dfrac{3}{2}\pi^2 r^3 = 40.9\,\mathrm{cm^3}$

1...................(A1)   which is a mass of $40.9 \times 0.275 \approx 11\,\mathrm{g}$

Total: 35 marks   **Other methods reaching the correct solution gain full marks.**

The learning benefits of such an exercise are obvious, but are best summed up by the Head of Mathematics.'

'The revision packs produced by this class were some of the best pieces of work produced by them in the A Level course.'

My thanks to John Wickham, Head of Mathematics at Thomas Rotherham College, and to his students who allowed me to use this example.

Chapter Five

Classroom Organisation

Classroom Organisation

During any one day teachers will often use a wide variety of approaches all with the same classroom layout. I once heard a former Headteacher in Somerset describe this as

'...trying to bake a cake on a spit.'

In Chapter One, Preparing the Ground, I argued that classroom layout is an important factor in determining whether whole-class teaching can be integrated successfully with other teaching and learning approaches. Let us consider just some of the activities that teachers might engage in with their classes in any one day:

- Whole-class instruction using a blackboard, whiteboard or OHP.
- Discussion in pairs or in small groups (eg Snowball technique).
- Tutorial with small groups of students (clarifying, challenging, coaching, testing).
- Small group or independent activity using resources or equipment housed in the classroom.
- Problem-solving activities in groups.
- Silent reading, writing or thinking.

This selection of activities will make huge demands on the organisational skills of the teacher, and if use of IT and practical activity is added to this list then you begin to realise the importance of classroom layout. The choice of room arrangement is a very personal matter - *for those who have choice*. Many secondary teachers will be timetabled in a number of rooms where the arrangement has been decided by someone else and the movement of furniture will be time-consuming and disruptive. Some teachers will have their own classroom but will have little choice over layout because the room is full of fixed furniture (eg a science laboratory with fixed benches or islands).

The options that follow, therefore, will be not be open to all teachers and may not be appropriate for specialist areas such as Design and Technology, Physical Education, Science or Performing and Expressive Arts.

Rows of Desks

Consider first the layout traditionally associated with whole-class teaching.

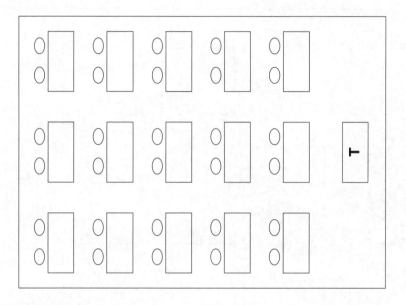

Plus points
- All students face the teacher.
- All students can see the blackboard.
- The teacher can see all students and can feel in control of behaviour.
- Techniques such as the Snowball are easy if one pair of students simply turn their chairs around to face the pair behind them.

Minus points
- Switching from this arrangement to group activity involves movement of furniture and resultant disruption.
- Discussion between the teacher and a student at the front is highly public.
- Small group tutorials will be difficult to organise.
- Students who move from the back to the front to collect resources sometimes interfere with or disrupt the work of others.
- Role-play will almost certainly involve re-arrangement of desks.

Group Tables

Many primary classroom will be arranged to reflect the frequent use of small groups for collaborative work.

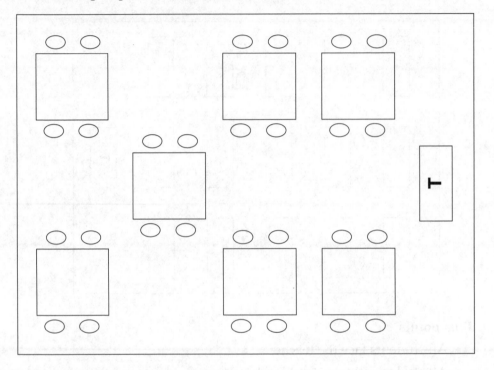

Plus points

- Students can provide support to each other (eg Support Groups).
- Small group discussion can be encouraged at any time.
- The teacher can join small groups at the table for tutorials.

Minus points

- Quiet work is difficult because there is usually one or more of the group keen to talk.
- Eye contact across the table often leads to distraction during quiet times or times when students should be listening.
- Teaching from the blackboard or OHP may lead to some students having their backs to the teacher.
- Individual work or testing is more difficult since the arrangement lends itself to collaboration.

The Horseshoe

Some teachers opt for unusual arrangements based on a circle, board room or horseshoe shape.

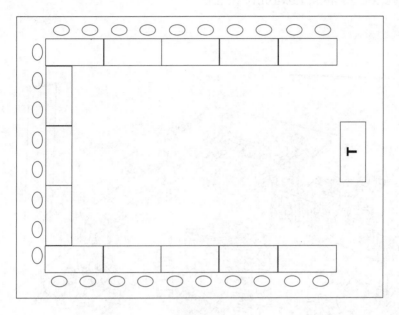

Plus points

- Good for control - the teacher can see all students in a way that is not possible in rows.
- The circular shape is more democratic and participation in class questioning is more likely than in rows.
- The shape is good for blackboard work.

Minus points

- Movement is difficult unless the room is unusually large.
- Such movement is highly visible - breaking the concentration of others.
- Group work involves a degree of movement and inevitable disturbance.
- Any discussion between the teacher and one student is highly public - 29 pairs of eyes can be off-putting to some students.
- Tutorials are difficult to organise.

The Periphery Approach

There is one arrangement that I first saw being used in the 1970s in a curriculum project in Bristol. It was highly innovative and, I believe, offers the greatest flexibility of all.

Screens in various sizes for use in classrooms as in the example are available from RBS Associates, Meadows House, Ampleforth Drive, Stafford, ST17 4TE. Tel: 01785 254859 Fax: 01785 220400

The students are grouped in 4s around two four foot tables pushed together and divided by a 4 foot square sheet of pinboard or corrugated plastic.

The boards are held up by the tables and can be removed in seconds and placed flat against the wall if group activity is needed.

Plus points

- Whole-class instruction is easy with the removal of the boards and the turning sideways of students' chairs.
- Teachers can move between quiet paired activity and group discussion in seconds without the need to move desks.
- Students now move to the middle to collect and return resources causing less disturbance to others.
- The screens act as a barrier both physically and emotionally - students like their own 'space'.
- The screens can be used for displaying visual information or resources (eg ordinance survey maps) or as a screen for hand-held slide projectors.
- The screens are superb for those occasions when tests are being conducted.
- The screens can be used to create private areas for reading, using IT or watching a video using headphones.

Minus points

- The boards need to be purchased.
- Placed wrongly the boards act as a visual screen preventing the teacher from monitoring behaviour.
- Many secondary teachers have to share classrooms and this arrangement may not suit everyone.
- Some classrooms with fixed furniture around the periphery will not permit this arrangement.
- Cheap pinboard will fray at the edges and can warp.

Many teachers who at first sight like this arrangement decide against it when they look more closely at their classrooms. For example, the classroom below would appear to have too much storage house around the walls for the periphery arrangement to be possible.

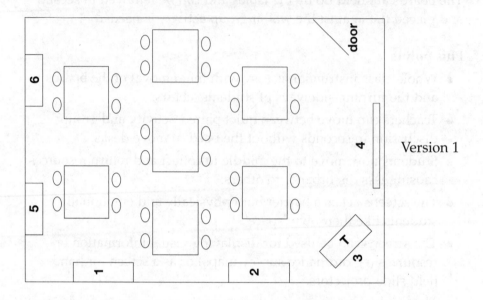

Version 1

A little re-arrangement, however, has made it possible.

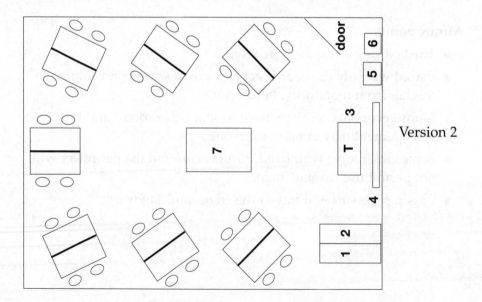

Version 2

In Version 2:

- The two four foot book cases (1 and 2) are now back to back and at right angles to the wall.
- The teacher's desk (3) is now in front of the blackboard (4) whereas before two spaces were needed.
- The cupboard (5) and filing cabinet (6) are now next to the blackboard.
- One wall is now being used for the storage and the teacher's desk instead of all four.
- The group tables and screens are angled so that all students are visible to the teacher at her desk.
- Two trolleys or tables (7) in the middle now house the resources that were formerly at the front.

Some teachers with no store cupboards but with storage units fixed to the walls will be reluctant to place tables in front of them because access is needed in all lessons. If, however, teachers are able to store those resources that are needed every lesson in one unit and those that are only needed periodically in another, then desks can still be placed in front of some cupboards.

Final Thoughts

Finally, I would advise teachers not to spend too much time worrying about the arrangement of furniture in the classroom until the need for flexible arrangements has been established. By far the most important task is to improve the quality of the teaching and learning. Once teachers have developed their confidence in using some of the strategies outlined in this book they will want to become more sophisticated in their use of classroom space. The re-arrangement of classrooms too early can divert attention from the key task of making whole-class teaching lively, interesting, enjoyable and effective.

References

Ausubal, D.   *The Use of Advanced Organisers in the*
                                        Learning and Retention of Meaningful
                                        Verbal Material.
                                        Journal of Educational Psychology,
                                        51, 1960.

Blagg N, et al   *Somerset Thinking Skills Course.*
                                        Basil; Blackwell, 1988.

De Bono, E.   *Cort Thinking*
                                        Pergamon 1986 (currently out of print)

Marland, M.   *The Craft of the Classroom*
                                        Heinemann 1993.

Parker, R.   *Looking Good in Print*
                                        Ventana Press 1993.

Powell, R.   *Raising Achievement*
                                        Robert Powell Publications 1997.

Smith, A.   *Accelerated Learning in the Classroom*
                                        Network Educational Press Ltd, 1996.

Waterhouse, P.   *Classroom Management*
                                        Network Educational Press Ltd, 1990.